TEEN

**Kimberly
Bolan Taney**

DISCARD

The Step-by-Step Library Makeover
SPACES

AMERICAN LIBRARY ASSOCIATION
Chicago   2003

Project editor: Joan A. Grygel

Printed on 50-pound white offset, a pH-neutral stock, and bound in 10-point coated cover stock by McNaughton & Gunn

The paper used in this publication meets the minimum requirements of American National Standard for Information Sciences—Permanence of Paper for Printed Library Materials, ANSI Z39.48-1992. ∞

Library of Congress Cataloging-in-Publication Data
Taney, Kimberly Bolan.
    Teen spaces : the step-by-step library makeover / Kimberly Bolan Taney.
       p.   cm.
    Includes bibliographical references and index.
    ISBN 0-8389-0832-2
    1. Libraries—Space utilization. 2. Young adults' libraries—Planning. 3. Library decoration.   I. Title.
    Z679.55.T36 2002
    022'.3—dc21   2002009122

Printed in the United States of America

07   06   05   04   03   5   4   3   2   1

Contents

Figures

Acknowledgments

Teen Spaces: The Step-by-Step Library Makeover was truly a joint venture of many wonderfully talented people. My gratitude goes out to all those who contributed their time and energy. Thanks to each of you for sharing your knowledge, experiences, and support. Without you this book would not be possible.

Renée Vaillancourt encouraged me to write my first book and had confidence in my abilities and in what I had to say.

Cathy Henderson was a fabulous friend and research assistant .

Judy Bassett provided hours of assistance, friendship, and "school library" input.

Over the years I've benefited greatly from the advice and experiences of my mentors. Lisa Wemett introduced me to the wonderful world of young adult services and teen spaces. Her guidance, continued faith in me, and input into this book were invaluable. Elly Dawson encouraged me to become a librarian and showed me, when I was 17 years old, that librarians were (and still are) cool people. Jennifer Morris took the time to make those "just to check up on you" phone calls. Many thanks to each of you for your support throughout the years.

My friends and coworkers at the Webster Public Library were all wonderfully supportive throughout the year, especially Marvin Andrews.

Thanks to Don Killaby at FJF Architects and to the authors and publishers who so graciously allowed me to reprint their work.

My friends and colleagues on the References and Adult Services Section of the New York State Library Association deserve thanks for listening and sticking by me.

My parents, Linda and Jim Bolan; my sister, Nicky; and my sister-in-law, Chris, constantly encouraged me. My brother, Ted Bolan, spent endless hours scanning and cropping photos and putting up with me in general.

My husband, Sean, endured the past year of boring (and sometimes quite stressful) weekends and, most importantly, brought me lunches from the Yankee Clipper so I could keep working without interruption.

Special thanks go to all the very talented librarians and their staffs who contributed information for this book.

Lastly, thanks to *all* the teens who took part in this project, especially Naomi Bacus, Aubrey Bendix, Kasey Bliek, Maggie Burgess, Meredith Chappell, Colleen Crispino, Luke Decker, Stacy Dupuis, Shannon Evans, Shannon Griepsma, Emily Hamilton, Carissa Herry, Sarah Hodges, Katie Keifer, Matthew Kwiatkowski, Sarah Landgrebe, Joe Militello, Dorothy Morehouse, Caitlin Mundy, Brenna O'Toole, Julie Provo, Dana Randisi, Alexis Romeo, Cassidy Stevens, Jessica Truax, John Weinert, and Albert Yin and to Micah Militello, who made a fantastic teen research assistant. You're all an inspiration.

Preface

Teenagers today long to be needed, to be respected, and to belong, and libraries are the ideal places for these things to happen. By creating a space designed especially for teens, librarians present themselves with the perfect opportunity to embrace this age group full force. With the worldwide population of teens quickly rising, libraries can no longer afford to give attention to everyone and every room in the library except teens and the teen area. Teenagers deserve a place to hang out, do homework, and be themselves. By recognizing teens as important "customers" today, libraries will ensure their adult patronage tomorrow.

Take a long, hard look at your library's teen space. What message does it send to teens? Does it uphold the traditional library stereotype—boring, unattractive, or even worse, nonexistent? A library's young adult space tells its teenagers a great deal about how you feel about them, and the stereotypical teen space simply tells them you do not care. It is not an easy task to dispel the boring, out-of-date, and unfriendly image of libraries, but with a little work, this can quickly change so that teens can see firsthand that a library is an exciting, "cool," and welcoming place to be.

Teen Spaces will help public and school librarians alike successfully plan and implement dynamic spaces for teens. Addressing the needs of a full range of library facilities of all shapes and sizes, this book is a practical, step-by-step guide to understanding teenagers and their "space" and the details of space planning, presenting plans to decision makers, effectively and creatively designing and decorating a teen space, and keeping teens interested long after the final coat of paint has dried. To make this process as easy as possible, market research on what teens want, ready-to-use forms, low-cost makeover ideas, and photographs of outstanding spaces are also included. Note that the sample photographs don't include teens. Not because the spaces don't get used but because presenting the photos in this manner allows you to focus simply on the spaces and their features.

Designing the ideal teen space might seem like an overwhelming task at first, especially if you're in a small or medium-sized library where staffing is at a premium, but it's not an impossible task. *Teen Spaces* is designed to be useful in any school or public library environment, so you can begin the process by picking and choosing what is applicable to your situation. Those who have smaller libraries might decide to start at a slower pace by referring to the sections that provide quick-and-easy makeover ideas. For instance, no one says you *have to* create a huge elaborate plan before taking action. If resources are limited, try rearranging what you have and incorporating a few flea market finds spruced up by a group of teens. You cannot accomplish everything at once, so glean what you can, focusing on one or two aspects at a time. On the other hand, for those who have a large facility, don't lose a great opportunity to start from scratch. You have the time and the resources. Evaluate what you have, create a master plan, and design a space that really "wows" teens. No matter what your situation, always tackle your biggest needs, concerns, or problems first, and gradually build from there. With a little thoughtful planning, an open mind, and a sense of adventure, you and your library will be well on your way to creating the "ideal" space for teens.

An emphasis of *Teen Spaces* is the young adult involvement, including specific ideas to get teens involved throughout the planning, development, and implementation stages. Teens will be your biggest and best resource. When young people are involved in creating and revamping a space, they will be more likely to accept and use the library. It will feel like it is theirs. In fact, when writing this book I created the teen spaces advisory council. Members performed a variety of duties including attending discussion groups, assisting with research, generating ideas, and compiling data. As with the development of a teen area, by including teenagers firsthand in the book, the final product instantly became stronger. Their ideas and input play a critical role in relaying information to you that is practical and achievable, rather than idealistic and unattainable. Look for the TIPs (*Teen Involvement Pointers*) features throughout the book to spot ways to get teens involved from start to finish. You won't be disappointed.

The Garfield Branch Library in Santa Cruz, California, stated the lessons it learned after completing its 1995 teen space project:

> When young people are involved in creating and revising service, they are likely to accept and use the library, and will be more willing to contribute time and energy to its operation. Just as important, the staff and the young adults come to understand each other in more than a superficial way, and from that understanding comes mutual respect.[1]

Teen involvement is the key element in the success of any school or public library's service to young adults. Get them involved in any way possible.

Over the last ten years I have worked in almost every type of library and library position imaginable: page, clerk, teen librarian, reference librarian, young adult consultant, network librarian, public librarian, school library assistant, and academic librarian. The one thing I took with me to each of these experiences was the lesson I learned early on in my career—all library users are important. It is this lesson that has led to my work with teenagers. Even in my current position as a network services and audiovisual librarian, I still include the teen perspective in everything I do. How could I not, especially when computers and AV are two of their specialties? No matter what job I tackle, I can't get away from the fact that teenagers are a great resource with many wonderful things to share and, without the input of *all* of my users, I would not be doing my job. This book is the result of a strong feeling about helping teenagers and my colleagues. I hope that by sharing my experiences working with teens and designing teen spaces I will help you to simply and easily create the ideal space for your teen patrons.

So, set your sights high, and don't be afraid to dream. It's our job to convince teenagers that libraries are wonderful welcoming places.

NOTE

1. *A Place of Our Own: Developing Effective Library Service for Young Adults* (Santa Cruz, Calif.: Garfield Branch Library). Available 63.193.16.16/grant_manual/toc.html (6 May 2001).

> For more images of exemplary and innovative library teen spaces see the Teen Spaces web site at
>
> http://www.ala.org/editions/teenspaces

Teens and Their Space 1

The first rule in design—before any plans are drawn up or one piece of furniture is moved—is to make sure you understand the customer. In the world of professional design, successful design projects are inherently the result of the designer having a firm grasp on customer needs and wants. In the case of libraries, responsive design of young adult areas comes from the librarian/designer understanding the group he or she is working to serve—teenagers. Learning to recognize teen behavior and needs, their likes and dislikes, is essential in understanding what is necessary and appropriate for the ideal young adult area.

Who Are Young Adults?

Who are teens exactly? How can you, as the librarian/designer, determine what their needs and wants are? According to Peter Zollo, author of *Wise Up to Teens: Insights into Marketing and Advertising to Teenagers,* the marketing world has defined the teen years as beginning at age twelve. Its members range in age from twelve to nineteen, including everyone from children just entering middle school to young adults attending college or holding down jobs. Research trends indicate that there are currently 31 million people age twelve to nineteen in the United States today and that this number will continue to expand, reaching an estimated 34 million by the year 2010.[1] The uniqueness of this group's size, as well as the group's diversity by gender, ethnicity, household income, geography, attitudes, and lifestyles, most definitely make it a challenging crowd to target. But, as Zollo reminds us, the rewards for doing so successfully are well worth the effort. The sizable numbers of teens are a clear indication that there is a population out there in need of attention, the services libraries offer, and a space designated just for them.

Ann Curry and Ursula Schwaiger summed it up best in their article on planning library spaces for teenagers:

> Teenagers have never been easy to understand. They straddle both
> childhood and adulthood, their minds and bodies filled with a restless

energy as they hurtle through developmental milestones at an amazing rate, yet each speed is uniquely personal. They are filled with an amazing power, yet are often crippled by anxiety and self-doubt.[2]

Now, take a look at figure 1.1 to see how teenagers describe this time in their lives.

FIGURE 1.1
The Best Words to Describe Being a Teenager

Pluses	*Minuses*
Top Three Answers:	**Top Three Answers:**
1. fun	1. difficult
2. freedom	2. frustrating
3. (tie) cool, friends, and exciting	3. (tie) annoying, busy, emotional, painful, confusing, and stressful
Other answers:	**Other answers:**
great experiences	repressed
super cool	messy
different	mad
involved	strange
expression	angry
creativity	surprising
changing	stupid
wonderful	embarrassing
interesting	repetitive
laughter	wary
energetic	contradictory
joyful	jam-packed
caring	tense
ecstatic	experimental
happy	confusing
crazy	bored
learning	sad
individual	exhausting
exhilarating	hectic
zany	feeling like a loser
philosophical	cynical
religious	smelly
challenging	more getting in trouble
brilliant	misunderstood
time of learning	
exciting	
time of growth	
weird	
new	
humorous	

Adjectives and descriptive phrases such as those in figure 1.1 provide a good initial picture of the group as a whole. This is definitely not a one-dimensional crowd. Most adults would agree that growing up was not easy and that being a teenager was one of the most difficult times of their lives, filled with a whirlwind of vastly differing experiences and emotions.

Youth development is defined as the ongoing process that prepares young people to meet challenges of adolescence and adulthood through a coordinated, progressive series of activities and experiences that help them become socially, morally, emotionally, physically, and cognitively competent.[3] The Center of Youth Development Policy Research has identified seven developmental needs of adolescents:

1. self-definition and independence
2. physical activity
3. creative expression
4. positive social interactions with peers and adults
5. competence and achievement
6. structure and clear limits
7. meaningful participation[4]

These needs can be fully met in a well-planned, full service teen library. For instance, to achieve self-definition and full independence, teens need and want a space of their own; one that is away from adults and little children. *Libraries can do this.* In conjunction with physical activity, teens need spaces and furniture that help them relax and move and stretch with their growing bodies. *Libraries can do this.* They need the opportunity to creatively express themselves and participate in projects that allow them to be imaginative, expressing their feelings and interests. *Libraries can do this.* Teenagers want and need a place where they can hang out with their friends and also experience positive interactions with adults. *Libraries can do this.* Teens want their contributions recognized and want to receive praise for their ideas and hard work. *Libraries can do this.* Finally, they need structure and clear limits. *Libraries can do this, too.* By building the ideal teen space and actively involving teens in the entire process, you are acting as their advocate, working to create a place with the potential for fulfilling all of their needs.

Over the last years, an independent, nonprofit organization, the Search Institute, has been striving to understand teens and their developmental needs. Its key finding is that the more assets adolescents have, the less likely they are to participate in dangerous behaviors and the more likely they are to engage in positive activities. The Search Institute's research, in particular the 1990 introduction of the forty developmental assets, shown in figure 1.2, has been of the greatest assistance to those serving teenagers. These assets have been identified as "the positive experiences, relationships, opportunities, and personal qualities that young people need to grow up healthy, caring, and responsible."[5]

The forty assets are divided into external assets and internal assets and then separated into eight categories. Look at the list of assets carefully, and determine which ones can be applied to your design project. Pay close attention to assets

FIGURE 1.2

Forty Developmental Assets

	CATEGORY	ASSET NAME AND DEFINITION
External Assets	Support	1. **Family support**—Family life provides high levels of love and support.
		2. **Positive family communication**—Young person and her or his parent(s) communicate positively, and young person is willing to seek advice and counsel from parent(s).
		3. **Other adult relationships**—Young person receives support from three or more nonparent adults.
		4. **Caring neighborhood**—Young person experiences caring neighbors.
		5. **Caring school climate**—School provides a caring, encouraging environment.
		6. **Parent involvement in schooling**—Parent(s) are actively involved in helping young person succeed in school.
	Empowerment	7. **Community values youth**—Young person perceives that adults in the community value youth.
		8. **Youth as resources**—Young people are given useful roles in the community.
		9. **Service to others**—Young person serves in the community one hour or more per week.
		10. **Safety**—Young person feels safe at home, school, and in the neighborhood.
	Boundaries and Expectations	11. **Family boundaries**—Family has clear rules and consequences and monitors the young person's whereabouts.
		12. **School boundaries**—School provides clear rules and consequences.
		13. **Neighborhood boundaries**—Neighbors take responsibility for monitoring young people's behavior.
		14. **Adult role models**—Parent(s) and other adults model positive, responsible behavior.
		15. **Positive peer influence**—Young person's best friends model responsible behavior.
		16. **High expectations**—Both parent(s) and teachers encourage the young person to do well.
	Constructive Use of Time	17. **Creative activities**—Young person spends three or more hours per week in lessons or practice in music, theater, or other arts.
		18. **Youth programs**—Young person spends three or more hours per week in sports, clubs, or organizations at school and/or in community organizations.
		19. **Religious community**—Young person spends one hour or more per week in activities in a religious institution.
		20. **Time at home**—Young person is out with friends "with nothing special to do" two or or more nights per week.
Internal Assets	Commitment to Learning	21. **Achievement motivation**—Young person is motivated to do well in school.
		22. **School engagement**—Young person is actively engaged in learning.
		23. **Homework**—Young person reports doing at least one hour of homework every school day.
		24. **Bonding to school**—Young person cares about her or his school.
		25. **Reading for pleasure**—Young person reads for pleasure three or more hours per week.
	Positive Values	26. **Caring**—Young person places high value on helping other people.
		27. **Equality and social justice**—Young person places high value on promoting equality and reducing hunger and poverty.
		28. **Integrity**—Young person acts on convictions and stands up for her or his beliefs
		29. **Honesty**—Young person "tells the truth even when it is not easy."
		30. **Responsibility**—Young person accepts and takes personal responsibility.
		31. **Restraint**—Young person believes it is important not to be sexually active or to use alcohol or other drugs.
	Social Competencies	32. **Planning and decision-making**—Young person knows how to plan ahead and make choices.
		33. **Interpersonal competence**—Young person has empathy, sensitivity, and friendship skills.
		34. **Cultural competence**—Young person has knowledge of and comfort with people of different cultural/racial/ethnic backgrounds.
		35. **Resistance skills**—Young person can resist negative peer pressure and dangerous situations.
		36. **Peaceful conflict resolution**—Young person seeks to resolve conflict nonviolently.
	Positive Identity	37. **Personal power**—Young person feels he or she has control over "things that happen to me."
		38. **Self-esteem**—Young person reports having a high self-esteem.
		39. **Sense of purpose**—Young person reports that "my life has a purpose."
		40. **Positive view of personal future**—Young person is optimistic about her or his personal future.

Reprinted with permission © Search Institute (Minneapolis, MN: Search Institute), 2001. www.search-institute.org.

such as community values youth, youth as resources, planning and decision making, and interpersonal competence. How could these be incorporated into the overall plan? Taking this approach will surely shine a new light on your plans. What may have started out as a project with the potential to increase library business could quickly develop into something even more worthwhile—something good for adolescents.

At first it might appear that creating a successful space for such a diverse group with so many needs is easier said than done. However, it's not as difficult as it seems. The key is to remember that your teen space doesn't have to be accomplished overnight and single-handedly. The process will take careful planning and time. Although you will serve as the driving force behind the project, you and your teen assistants will carry it through to the end. Teenagers are the biggest and best resource for the job.

Understanding Teen Wants and Needs

To start figuring out what teens are all about, consider their pastimes, friends, and personal preferences. Begin by brainstorming the answers to a few fundamental questions:

- What activities do teens primarily do?
- Where do they prefer to hang out and why?
- What or who is genuinely important to them?

Start by envisioning what it was like for you as a teen. Then, think about what it's like being a teen today. What are your perceptions and assumptions? Validate your thoughts, and find out how things realistically compare by browsing through a resource such as Peter Zollo's *Wise Up to Teens: Insights into Marketing and Advertising to Teenagers*. (See appendix B.) Zollo's book provides real-life examples and gives you an understanding of teen attitudes, values, and lifestyles.

Finally, after reflecting on these questions, begin thinking about how to apply the answers to the design plan. For example, if hanging out with friends is what is important to teens, how could that be incorporated into the design of the teen area? If it's conclusive that the mall and sporting events are high on their list of where they prefer to hang out, how could you best use that information? Keep in mind that the thought process behind the answers is equally as important as the answers themselves because making the effort and taking the time to try to think like a teenager gives an adult important insight into a teen's world and allows for a better end result.

Market Research

To really *know* teenagers you need to find out what they're saying about their likes, dislikes, wants, and needs. Conducting thorough market research will help you understand your young adult patrons and will ultimately assist in creating an identity for your teen space, its products, and its services. Market research commonly involves gathering primary and secondary data. The majority of the information will be of the secondary variety, already compiled and organized for you. Examples include reports and studies such as those presented by Peter Zollo in *Wise Up to Teens* and by Elissa Moses in *The $100 Billion Allowance: Assessing the Global Teen Market*. Primary data involves carrying out your own market research through written, online, telephone, and in-person surveys or conducting discussion groups, observing teens, and having one-on-one conversations. (More information on conducting your own market research is in chapter 2.)

Throughout the market research process, keep in mind that when it comes to talking to teens, the key lies in direct and open communication—really hearing what they have to say and sincerely making an effort to relate to them. Raymond O'Neal, CEO of Threshold Media Ventures in New York, says that when he was first starting his career gathering information about teen apparel, his best results came when he made the effort to relate to teens, looking the way they looked. He wore the same clothing, hung out with them, and found out what teens wanted. O'Neal reveals, "Consumers will accept advice from someone they can trust. For example, they are more likely to take a handout at a mall if they can relate to the person who is handing it out."[6]

Observation

Another excellent way to gather information and begin understanding your teenaged customers is to familiarize yourself with their environments including their school lockers, school hallways, the mall, and favorite hangouts. Figure 1.3 shows what the *Teen Spaces* advisory council observed in the lockers of students in six schools in upstate New York in 2001. Careful observation of the things, places, and people that teens surround themselves with reveals a great deal about their nature, personality, likes, and dislikes. For instance, if you know that the majority of teens ages 13 to 18 have mirrors, beauty products, snacks, and CD players in their lockers, what does this tell you? How can you use this information to develop an effective young adult space plan? It says that appearance, food, and music are important to this age group. Knowing this, it would be wise for libraries to

concentrate on both teen music and beauty/fitness collections, keeping them up-to-date and easily accessible

incorporate listening stations or a stereo into the teen area

allow teens to eat snacks and drink in the library

hang a mirror in the teen area for quick hair and makeup checks

The main point is to make a few observations and to see the correlation between teen surroundings and how they can influence the design of a teen area.

Surveys

If you *really* want to find out more about teens and their preferences, just ask them directly. You can do this by randomly talking to them one on one, conducting

FIGURE 1.3
What's in a Teenager's Locker

Girls' Lockers	Boys' Lockers
School supplies	School supplies
Garbage	Clothes
Clothes	Random pictures
Beauty products	Sports equipment
Decorations	Food
Food/drinks	Old homework and tests
Pictures of friends	CD players and CDs
Mirrors	Garbage
Magnets	Strange odds and ends
Hair accessories	Beauty products
Personal hygiene products	(gel, cologne, mirrors)
Stuffed animals/toys	Magazine pictures
Magazine clippings	Pictures of friends
Sports equipment	Writing, graffiti, quotes
CD players	Backpacks
Pictures of males	Basketball hoops
Calendars	Drawings
Gum	Money
Jewelry	Keys
Keys	
Photographs	
Purses/bags	
Writing utensils	
Coffee	
Poetry	
Cell phones	
Eraser boards	

TIP

If you *really* want to find out more about teens and their preferences, just ask them directly. You can do this by randomly talking to them one on one, conducting surveys, and forming teen committees and advisory groups.

surveys, and forming teen committees and advisory groups. (For more details on conducting surveys and creating teen focus groups and advisory boards, refer to chapter 2.) Getting teen input is critical to the entire design process. Teenagers are the ones who can honestly (and be prepared for complete truthfulness) tell you the impression your library is making (or not making) on them. In fact, much of the information presented in this book was gathered directly from teens using a combination of each of these techniques.

Survey Results

If you ask them, teens will be more than willing to tell you what is necessary to get them to hang out. Teens surveyed between November 1998 and May 1999 in communities serving ten public libraries across the United States indicated that they would like to see the following items in their libraries:

a place of their own (i.e., a teen area)

bright, cheerful colors and objects

quiet study area

place to socialize

comfortable furniture

music area

video room

performance space

updated technology, more computers in general,
    and better quality hardware and software

food and drinks (vending machines, snack bars, etc.)

more people their own age and fewer adults

clean, up-to-date materials with clearer arrangement

better customer service for students

longer weekend and evening hours

variety of activities[7]

In addition to these essentials, the *Teen Spaces* advisory council recommended the following:

lots of magazines

large selection of audiovisual materials

good fiction collection

notebook/laptop computers that can be checked out

television or a video preview room

VCR and DVD player

friendly, up-to-date staff

How can these insights help develop your library's space plan? How do they influence your ideas and goals?

In general, teenagers say that a good teen area must be welcoming, fun, exciting, clearly defined, attractive, and informal. Its contents must be up-to-date, functional, easy to arrange, and durable. A first-rate teen space should have the ability to fit into a teen's social life; that is, a teen area must include space for its patrons to congregate and talk and giggle. At its best, a young adult area should be designed so that there is no mistake that the area was created especially for teenagers. Just as teens long for separate identities, it is equally important for them to establish a distinct area that allows them to express their individuality.

The Teen Space

After you have a general understanding of your teen customers, start looking into the physical space itself, examining those essential components such as location, function, content, staffing, and layout. This will help you form preliminary ideas and supply the initial framework for the project. Such components will also provide the basic information necessary for building the foundation of the space plan (see chapters 2 and 3) and, ultimately, pulling together the ideal teen area (see chapters 4 and 5).

Location

Your choice of location could conceivably make or break a teen space, so put careful thought and analysis into your needs because choosing the right location for your teen area could be one of the most important decisions you make. Consider the following factors:

- the customers and their specific needs
- traffic patterns and accessibility
- appearance of the area

Taking these into consideration, the ideal location of a teen space should have the following advantages:

easy accessibility with good traffic flow (Teens should be able to discern their area when first walking through the front doors. This can be done by locating the teen area near the entrance of the library or by using signage that quickly points them in the right direction.)

high visibility with some degree of privacy (The location should be near all the "key" areas such as reference, computers, etc., but also fairly secluded so teens have the freedom to talk without disturbing others.)

flexibility, incorporating room for future growth

When at all possible, try to avoid putting the teen area next to the children's room. Teenagers do not want to be associated with the "children's" area, so putting them in the vicinity of preschoolers would strategically be a bad move. By the same token, positioning the young adult area near or next to areas to which they need access, such as the reference desk, nonfiction area, and magazines or audiovisual areas, would be a smart move. Choose a location that won't completely isolate teens from the rest of the library and take into consideration the impact the teen space will have on other patrons and areas of the library.

Issues such as sight lines from the teen space to the circulation and reference desks for observational purposes and what determines when an area has too much privacy raise questions and legitimate concerns. Although you want teens to have fun, freedom, and the opportunity to socialize, you do not want these areas to turn into a party zone It's essential to keep *all* of these things in mind when choosing a location.

Although there really isn't one perfect location for a teen area, keep in mind the guidelines set forth in this section and incorporate them into what works best in your library environment and suits your teen patrons' needs. Always compare the strengths and weaknesses of several locations before making a final decision.

Function

A key rule to keep in mind throughout the planning and design process is that form follows function. Having a solid grasp on how teens use the library and on how the young adult area will ultimately operate will help you better plan the aesthetics of the space. Whether choosing a location, purchasing furniture and materials, or laying out the space, all design elements will ultimately come back to the question of, "What best supports the functions of the space?"

To get started, make a list of all the activities planned for the new young adult area. Include everything you can think of including studying, socializing, meetings, after-school activities, reference assistance, programs (small group and large group), etc. Once you have generated the list, determine what will be needed in the physical space to accommodate such activities. Will you need to consider "multiple" spaces (i.e., a reading area and a lounging area, a separate meeting room, an office space for teen staff, etc.)? These are more pieces of the puzzle that will help you shape the space and the overall direction of the project.

Inevitably, considering the functions of the space will raise questions that will lead to answers that will point you in the right direction. For instance, you might ask, "Should a teen area be for educational purposes or for entertainment?" and "Should it serve as a quiet study area or a central meeting place?" At its best, the ideal teen area should not be limited to only one purpose or role; instead it should serve as a multifunctional space: for studying, hanging out, socializing, meeting after school, typing papers, using the Internet, listening to music, being entertained, getting help with homework, reading, or simply relaxing. All libraries must strive to build such a space for their teen patrons; however, some libraries will have more freedom, funding, space, and flexible management than others do. The most important thing to remember is that anyone can have a teen space that is "everything" to its teenagers as long as the planners keep open minds and have a willingness to try. The key is to include as many functions as possible for each library's situation, and the rest will fall into place.

Content

The content of a young adult area includes all those items that will assist in defining the physical space. Fundamentals include

> furniture and fixtures (tables, chairs, couches, shelves, display units, accessories)
>
> the collection, including materials of all formats (books, audiovisual items, magazines, etc.)
>
> equipment (computers, printers, listening devices, e-book readers, etc.)
>
> signage
>
> any other physical components of the area

Begin to create a list of items you envision in the space. What items can be derived from the function list? For example, if a function of the area is that it will be used for hanging out after school, then this will determine what kinds of furniture you'll consider. This function might also suggest purchasing more "browseable" materials, such as graphic novels and magazines, or looking into incorporating music listening stations or stereo equipment into the area. If a function will be to provide computer access and assistance on a regular basis, then this would imply additional computer purchases for the space and improved literature and signage to show where teens could find help.

Staff

The element of staffing is not always as evident as the other components, but it is equally as important. Just as shelving, carpeting, and books are a part of a new space, so are people. Analyzing the staffing situation beforehand will enhance the final space plan. A library's staffing situation will guide both the location and the layout of a teen area. After all, staff will be the ones responsible for working with teens and maintaining and promoting young adult services.

From day one of the project, take into account who will be involved with the space when it's fully functional. For example, a small or medium-sized public library is less likely than a school library or large public library to have a separate help desk staffed by a young adult specialist. In all instances decisions must be made that will shape the space plan. For a small public library, a decision about where to locate key service points in relation to the entire teen area will be crucial. In a school or large public library, the decision of where to best locate the service desk within the space and how to staff it as many hours as possible will be a guiding factor. In all situations it's vital that staff members be readily accessible to teens so there is no question about where they can find help. It is also important that staff who will assist teen patrons be friendly, approachable, and knowledgeable. In all actuality, a library can be stylishly decorated and filled with great materials, but if the staff is unapproachable and rude, teens won't want to use the area. Thinking about your library's staffing situation at the beginning of the project, rather than at the end, will be one of the best moves you will make in developing your young adult space.

Layout

The foremost thing to remember when discussing layout is that it's not the amount of floor space a library has, it's what you do with the space that matters. The smallest of library spaces can be the most creative, well-designed places for teens as long as they are arranged with careful consideration to its users and functions. After you have determined a location for your teen area and thought through the function, content, and staffing situation, obtain a floor plan of the entire library as well as an enlarged plan of the teen area. A good floor plan shows the entire area and the space that each piece of furniture occupies. Floor plans provide a perspective of how things currently exist and how they are arranged and will serve as an invaluable tool and visual aid throughout the design process. If a professionally drawn floor plan is not available, create a simplified version. (See chapters 2 and 4 for more details and sample plans.)

Start the layout analysis by looking for *potential.* Examine all the possibilities for the space by taking into account each of the key components (location, function, content, and staff) and how they tie together. Each will have a significant effect on the ultimate presentation of the space. Additional elements to consider include

> access, that is, smooth traffic flow and handicap accessibility (i.e., space between aisles, the height of study carrels and tables, etc.) (See appendix B for resources on obtaining a copy of *ADA Standards for Accessible Design.*)
>
> logical arrangement of and easy access to all materials (see chapter 5)
>
> equipment placement that is easy to locate by teens as well as easy to monitor by staff (refer to chapter 4)
>
> decorating elements including lighting, signage, and wall treatments (refer to chapter 4)

As the design process progresses, use the floor plan to manipulate the layout to reflect new ideas and proposed changes for the space.

Everyone faces similar questions and concerns when starting to examine their young adult areas. In essence, you need to get a firm idea of what teens want and need by communicating with them and, ultimately, relating to them throughout the design process. The design elements will fall into place once you clearly understand the group for which the area is being designed. Ideas and plans may change many times, but that is all part of the process. Take plenty of time and give careful consideration to any and all ideas. Although the following chapters will provide step-by-step basics for designing the ideal young adult area, appreciating the importance of teenagers and recognizing their uniqueness will be the best resource for discovering the key to creating and maintaining a winning teen space.

Notes

1. Peter Zollo, *Wise Up to Teens: Insight into Marketing and Advertising to Teenagers* (Ithaca, N.Y.: New Strategist Publications, 1999): 21.

2. Ann Curry and Ursula Schwaiger, "The Balance between Anarchy and Control: Planning Library Space for Teenagers," *School Libraries in Canada* 19, 1 (1999): 9.

3. National Youth Development Information Center (Washington, D.C.). Available www.nydic.org/devdef.html (23 Nov. 2001).

4. Dr. Peter Scales, "Creating a Developmental Framework: The Positive Possibilities of Young Adolescents," in *A Portrait of Young Adolescents in the 1990s* (Minneapolis, Minn.: Search Institute Center for Early Adolescence, 1991). Available www.search-institute.org (10 May 2001).

5. The Search Institute, "Developmental Assets: An Overview." Available www.search-institute.org (23 Nov. 2001).

6. Raymond O'Neal Jr., "Ten Commandments of Urban Marketing," Available www.ddimagazine.com (8 Sept. 2001).

7. Elaine Meyers, "The Coolness Factor: Ten Libraries Listen to Youth," *American Libraries* (30 Nov. 1999): 42.

Ask and Analyze

2

Start your design project by talking with teens and staff. Teenagers are your target customers (the users), and staff members are the ones who will be behind the scenes carrying out the plan (the supporters). It's important not to waste valuable time and energy devising a plan based only on your assumptions. Instead, let staff and teens guide you. Ask them openly for their ideas. Their comments and suggestions will be valuable in sorting out your preliminary ideas and establishing concrete goals and objectives for the project. Next, move on to the second phase—the space analysis. This is where you begin to gather tangible data that will be used to support your goals and objectives by measuring and comparing library services and statistics and by taking a complete inventory of the existing space. In the end, the information gathered by following the procedures in this chapter will become the foundation for your space plan.

Those Involved

Communication is an essential component of the design process. It involves not only relaying information but, more importantly, listening. Getting input from teens and library staff will prove invaluable throughout the project. Brainstorming sessions, surveys, advisory groups, and Junior Friends of the Library are a few simple ways to actively involve key players while at the same time gathering valuable information.

TIP

Brainstorming sessions, surveys, advisory groups, and Junior Friends of the Library are a few simple ways to actively involve key players while at the same time gathering valuable information.

Brainstorming Sessions

Brainstorming is a useful tool for gathering a myriad of ideas and perspectives in a short period of time. More importantly, it is an efficient way to collect ideas from both teens and staff members. Sessions should be conducted two or three times throughout the course of the planning and design stages.

Acknowledgment of staff input is critical in making this project work because they are the ones who will be responsible for supporting the new and improved teen space. Without the support of staff members, a well-intentioned teen project will quickly fail. The first staff brainstorming session should be held at the beginning of the project and include a combination of youth services staff as well as staff members from outside the department (three to five staff at maximum to begin). This session should be casual, nonthreatening, and informative for all involved. Begin by briefly describing the purpose behind the meeting and follow up with some ice-breaking questions such as "What was your worst experience with teens in the library?" and "What was your best experience with teens in the library?" Next, move on to ask the group key questions specifically related to the goal of creating a new and improved young adult area. Divide the discussion into two parts:

1. young adult services
2. physical young adult space

Refer to appendix A for a Brainstorming Ideas Worksheet. Sample topics are listed in an easy-to-use grid format to simplify organization and note taking. When using the brainstorming worksheet, formulate the discussion so that each topic is asked in three ways.

- Where has the library *been* in relation to _____?
- Where *should* the library be in relation to _____?
- Where is the library *headed* in relation to _____?[1]

This type of questioning will provide focus and direction for the group. Remember to set a time limit so that one topic does not monopolize the conversation. Consider meeting over the course of several sessions, tackling services in one meeting and physical space in another.

Throughout the discussions, encourage participants to be candid about their feelings regarding a new young adult area and be prepared to listen to a variety of opinions and viewpoints. It's better to get staff concerns out in the open at the beginning than to be surprised in the middle or, even worse, at the end of the project. Potential areas of concern might include things such as a shortage of staff and time, physical distance of the teen area from service desks for observational purposes, and the possibility of loud talking and rude behavior.

After brainstorming with staff, it is equally important to initiate a similar session with teens. Many of the questions developed for the staff brainstorming session can be applied to teen discussion groups. Participants for these sessions can be gathered in a number of ways, but the most effective and dependable method is to form a teen advisory board or a teen focus group early on in the project. (Guidelines for doing so are developed later in this chapter.) Once you've established a core group of teen assistants, there will be countless "brains to pick" from that moment on.

Teen Surveys

A simple and easy way to find out about teens and to generate ideas for your young adult area and services is to develop a survey. Teens love them. Surveys give teenagers the opportunity to voice their opinions. They are also an inexpensive and easy way to reach a large number of people at a variety of locations. Conduct surveys in writing, online, over the phone, or in-person.

Survey Design

When designing the survey, keep it simple and to the point. A survey that is too long won't be completed. With print surveys, the format must be eye-catching and visually appealing. Use clip art, attention-grabbing fonts (generally not more than two), and experiment with color. Be creative! Try to stick to multiple-choice questions as opposed to open-ended questions, but always leave room at the end for one open-ended question that invites comments or other ideas. Figure 2.1 shows a sample survey for teens.

TIP

Surveys give teenagers the opportunity to voice their opinions. They are also an inexpensive and easy way to reach a large number of people at a variety of locations.

Survey Availability

Next, you need to get the survey out there. You can accomplish this in a number of ways:

Distribute surveys in-house, asking participants to put completed forms in a suggestion box.

With an online survey, advertise to let teens know it's there. (See chapter 5 for more information on successful advertising.)

Hand out the surveys in person. (Make sure there is a convenient place for teens to leave completed forms.) With an online survey you might ask the computer lab instructors at school to tell teens about it, and ask the instructors if they would let students spend a few minutes of their time completing it.

FIGURE 2.1
Sample Teen Survey

We WANT to know... what YOU think!

1. Are you a ☐ male or a ☐ female?

2. How old are you? _____

3. How often do you use the library? (*Check one.*)
   ☐ Once a week ☐ Once a month
   ☐ Once a year ☐ Only when I have to
   ☐ What library? _____

4. Where do you like to hang out with friends?
   (*Check all that apply.*)
   ☐ At my house ☐ At their house
   ☐ Community Center
   ☐ Local hangout (What's it called?)
   _____
   ☐ School library ☐ Public Library
   ☐ Other_____
   _____

5. Where is your *favorite* place to study?
   ☐ My bedroom ☐ At a friend's house
   ☐ At school ☐ At the library
   ☐ Other _____
   Why?_____

6. Think of your most favorite place to be. What
   2 things make it your favorite place?
   a._____
   b._____

7. What kinds of things would you like to see in the
   library? (*Check all that apply.*)
   ☐ Music ☐ Stereo system
   ☐ Individual listening stations
   ☐ VCR ☐ Videos ☐ DVDs
   ☐ DVD player ☐ Computers
   ☐ Comfy furniture
   ☐ Comics/graphic novels ☐ Magazines
   ☐ Electronic games ☐ Board games
   ☐ Lots of good paperbacks
   ☐ Other_____

8. What 2 things would you *most* like to borrow
   from the library with your library card?
   ☐ Books (If so, what kinds of books (fantasy,
   mysteries, etc.)?_____
   ☐ Music CDs ☐ Videos
   ☐ DVDs ☐ CD-ROMs
   ☐ Books on cassette/CD
   ☐ Games
   ☐ Graphic novels/manga, etc.
   ☐ Other _____

9. What do you *like* to use computers for?
   ☐ Chat/IM ☐ E-mail ☐ Play games
   ☐ Look up fun stuff ☐ Download stuff
   ☐ Make web pages ☐ Type letters
   ☐ School research
   ☐ Other_____

10. What types of events and programs would you
    like to see at the library? (*Check your top 3.*)
    ☐ Sports/exercise ☐ Writing workshop
    ☐ Music ☐ Arts/crafts ☐ Book discussion
    ☐ Homework help ☐ Computer skills
    ☐ Dancing ☐ Babysitting
    ☐ Job hunting skills ☐ Movies
    ☐ Cartooning ☐ Other _____

11. What activities, subjects, or items are you abso-
    lutely passionate about? This can be anything
    from horses to soccer to science to music, and if
    you're not into anything, tell us that too. (*Please
    write on the back.*)

12. What suggestions do you have for attracting
    teens to the library? (*Please write on the back.*)

13. Would you be interested in serving on a teen
    council that helps design a space especially for
    you in the library? ☐ YES ☐ NO

    If YES . . .

    Name:_____

    Phone: _____

To get input from nonlibrary users, strategically place the paper survey around favorite hangouts such as the community center, pizza shop, etc. It is especially important to make the surveys exciting and interesting enough for teens to see them and to want to complete them. Remember to include instructions about where to hand in the surveys after they're complete, perhaps in a collection box on site where the surveys can be picked up weekly.

Complete surveys (paper or online) at group brainstorming/focus group sessions.

Go into the community and verbally survey teens. For example, the Lake Hills Library staff in Bellevue, Washington, went to the shopping mall, a transit bus stop heavily used by teens, a city teen council meeting, and a youth detention center. This is a great method for hearing from teens who do not use the library.

TIP

Consider putting a trustworthy teen in charge of gathering the surveys from the off-site collection boxes every few days or so. Depending on how comfortable you feel with the confidentiality of your survey and the reliability of the teens you involve in the survey collection, you might want to consider having some teens compile the results for you too.

Don't forget to set a time limit for distributing and collecting the surveys (two weeks is a reasonable time frame). The longer they're out there the more "invisible" they become. And don't be discouraged. If it doesn't work the first time, revamp the survey, rethink your distribution methods, and try it again. Consider putting a trustworthy teen in charge of gathering the surveys from the off-site collection boxes every few days or so. Depending on how comfortable you feel with the confidentiality of your survey and the reliability of the teens you involve in the survey collection, you might want to consider having some teens compile the results for you too.

Survey Results

Using the original survey as a master, compile results using the tally method. Record the number of responses for each question above the corresponding answer on the original survey. If you ask for responses to open-ended questions in the comments section at the end of the survey, list the comments exactly as worded and record them at the end of the compilation. For each answer, divide the number of responses by the number of teens who completed the survey. This will give you a percentage for each answer. (Note that the percentages for each answer should total 100 percent.) If time and resources allow, consider putting results into a spreadsheet to incorporate into your final plan. (Refer to chapter 3 for more details on developing a plan.) Post survey results on the library's web page as well as at the library to show teens that you take their comments seriously. Most importantly, share the survey results with your administrator, and incorporate these new and exciting ideas into your space plan.

Teen Advisory Boards, Focus Groups, and Junior Friends

Teens want to make a contribution to society, and they need a forum to provide input into those things that directly involve them. Forming a teen advisory board, implementing teen focus groups, or starting a Junior Friends of the Library are all excellent ways for libraries to get young adults involved. They are also great ways for teens to earn community service hours to fulfill graduation requirements. What could be better? Teens get their well-deserved input (and assistance in graduating), and the library benefits from their guidance and service.

A teen advisory board or council is generally a long-term group and is recommended for providing ongoing service for the young adult area and services. Teen boards tackle a myriad of topics such as advising on library rules and regulations, young adult collection development, and programming, including planning parties, writing original plays, conducting contests, etc. Their duties can also consist of raising money, volunteering for after-school activities and service projects (such as children's summer reading program and computer classes), and overseeing special ventures such as a teen space renovation. On average, advisory boards meet monthly, but the number and length of each meeting may vary depending on the tasks at hand.

A focus group is generally short-term and is formed to discuss and generate ideas related to a particular topic or topics. Basically, this is a teen-brainstorming group. Focus groups can be formed in addition to other teen groups, or they may serve as a temporary alternative to an advisory board. In fact, forming a focus group is also a great segue into establishing a teen board. Focus groups generally meet based on need (weekly, bimonthly, etc.), and the length of the meetings varies based on the topic at hand.

A Junior Friends of the Library (JFOL) group is quite similar in nature to a teen advisory board or council. The primary difference is that members of JFOL pay annual dues that must be renewed each year (generally $5 per year). The Union County Library of Lake Butler, Florida, also has a "supporting business" membership category that is open to any business or organization in the community interested in supporting the efforts of the group.[2] Annual membership dues are $20. Union County JFOL meetings are held on a monthly basis, conducted by the chairperson and run by *Robert's Rules of Order*. The Union County JFOL officers include the chairperson, a vice-chairperson, a secretary, and a treasurer. Officers are elected by a majority vote of all members. Although the Union County JFOL's activities and duties are similar in nature to those of a teen advisory board, the JFOL has more responsibility for fundraising (comparable to the efforts of an adult Friends group). Union County's JFOL raises money for new library materials as well as for a scholarship fund for annual awards to two deserving senior JFOL members.

Recruitment

Recruitment is key to making any teen group a success. Post signs throughout the library, distribute fliers, write a press release for the school paper or library newsletter or, better yet, approach teens directly. You'll also want to make an effort to work with colleagues in the community to target nonusers of the library. Network with teens you already know, get names of their friends, and send out e-mail notices or make a few phone calls.

Guidelines for Success

To ensure that your teen advisory board, focus group, or Junior Friends group is a success, keep the following in mind:

> Include a variety of ages (grades 7 through 12).
>
> Keep the group size of advisory boards and focus groups to a maximum of thirty teens or else the group becomes too unwieldy. (The more the merrier when it comes to Junior Friends.)
>
> Actively communicate with teens.
>
> Learn each teen's name and use it.
>
> Let teens know you are interested in their lives, their interests, and their friends and that they are important to you and the library.
>
> Encourage the entire library staff to be pro-teen.
>
> Bear in mind that teen groups are as unique as the personalities of the teens involved.
>
> Let teens do the work. (You provide the support.)
>
> When a teen completes a task, praise him or her, and if someone makes a mistake, don't reprimand him or her—everyone makes mistakes.[3]

Libraries that have had success with teen groups such as these include: Campbell County Public Library (Gillette, Wyoming), Chino Hills Branch Library (Chino Hills, California), Lake Hills Library (Bellevue, Washington), Lawrence Public Library (Lawrence, Kansas), the Leominster Public Library (Leominster, Massachusetts), Phoenix Public Library (Phoenix, Arizona), Schaumburg Township District Library (Schaumburg, Illinois), and Union County Public Library (Lake Butler, Florida), just to name a few. You may want to contact these or other libraries with teen groups listed in appendix C.

The Area

You have started gathering input from teens and staff, so the next step is to make a thorough analysis of your existing young adult facility. A successful young adult space analysis must address the following issues:

1. motivation—an explanation of the "drive" behind the project
2. comparison with other library areas—how young adult services stack up against the other departments/services, including general information pertaining to the area as well as a detailed comparison of the teen area with other areas of the library
3. a detailed inventory—an outline of the existing space's furnishings, fixtures, collection, etc.
4. layout—the floor plan of the existing space
5. a listing of strengths and weaknesses—the positives and negatives of the existing young adult space to help generate a needs assessment and list of priorities as you move into the planning stage

Each of these steps is crucial for organizing ideas and, ultimately, keeping the project on target. If clear and well thought out, the resulting analysis will provide the necessary framework for a teen space plan that is both well received and truly functional.

Motivation

What is the drive behind your young adult space project? Is the project an independent redesign introduced by the young adult or youth services department? If so, this type of endeavor is generally initiated because the current teen facility is nonexistent or in desperate need of improvement. Categorizing the project in this manner provides the necessary focus for your plan. When a young adult space project falls into the "independent redesign" category, the emphasis should be on building a persuasive plan compelling enough to convince decision makers that the project is a necessary and worthwhile endeavor meriting the investment of both library time and money. Your attention should focus on "selling" the idea.

If the project does not fall into the independent redesign category, then it is most likely a component of a larger undertaking such as a library building expansion or renovation. A large-scale project such as this is usually initiated by administration for the greater good of the entire library facility. When a teen space project falls under the umbrella of a bigger plan such as a new building project, it is a given that some sort of young adult space change will ultimately take place. The question now is, what kind of change will that be? In this instance it is up to the person in charge of young adult services to influence those decisions and changes. Space plans and proposals must have that "wow" factor that will convince administration that the teen area deserves as much (if not more) funding, space, and attention as the other areas of the library.

Teen Services Compared with Other Services

Begin this stage by noting fundamental information about the library as a whole. Include specifics such as population of service area, public service hours, door count (i.e., how busy the library is), staff (names, titles, and statuses), and the date the library was built. (This may directly coincide with the last known "update" in the teen area.) Also gather information about the collection sizes and circulation for each department. For comparison, collect similar data specifically related to young adult services and compare the numbers. Comparative data will prove essential when attempting to obtain support or funding for a project of this nature. Once it is clear how teen services rank in relation to the rest of the library, you will be able to gradually start building your plan. Use the young adult services Comparison Worksheet located in appendix A to assist you in this process. At this time you do not need to complete the last column of the Comparison Worksheet. It will be completed later in chapter 2. If the service population figures for children and young adults are not available, call your local school district for an estimate. How does the young adult collection compare with the other collections? Break it out into books, magazines, AV materials, online resources, etc., or whatever is appropriate for your situation. When looking at the library staffing statistics, you may want to list the names, titles, and statuses on another sheet of paper.

The Inventory

Taking an inventory involves evaluating the existing content of the teen area. Never make assumptions about what you "think" makes up the area. It's important that you check the space firsthand with a critical eye. If feasible, ask someone from outside the library (perhaps a colleague from another school or public library or someone from the local recreation department or a popular teen hangout) to view the space with you. You'd be surprised at the insight and perspective a fresh eye will bring to the project. Participation of members of a teen advisory board or teen focus group would be another excellent resource during the inventory analysis.

When working with teens during the inventory process, it is helpful to hand out a blank inventory checklist (see figure 2.2) to each person before walking through the teen area as a group. Use the inventory provided or modify it as needed. Briefly explain the sheet and what each person is expected to do. As the group progresses through the space, introduce the inventory components one at a time, giving each person time to jot down his or her initial reactions and ideas. If teens come across a component that they cannot address (i.e., filtered Internet access, staffing issues, etc.), tell them to skip it. Collect everyone's sheets. Get together a few days later, hand back the sheets, give each person a few minutes to review what he or she wrote, and open the floor to discussion. To keep things orderly, bring up one component at a time, and elect a secretary from the group to take note of and compile the findings produced by the group.

During the inventory process, it's essential to keep detailed records and write down as much information as possible. Use the Inventory Checklist as a guide (see figure 2.2). It is also important to keep in mind that a thorough inventory should include *what is not there* as well as what is. The following sections provide definitions of terms used in the inventory.

> **TIP**
>
> Participation of members of a teen advisory board or teen focus group would be another excellent resource during the inventory analysis.

FIGURE 2.2
Inventory Checklist

	Yes	No	N/A	Comments
A. Layout				
1. Is the young adult area a separate area?				
2. Is the building entrance nearby?				
3. Is there privacy?				
4. Can teens socialize without disturbing others?				
5. Is the young adult area near the children's room?				
Reference?				
Computers?				
(Describe where the young adult area is in relationship to other departments.)				
6. Is there adequate floor space devoted to young adults? (Describe how it relates to the entire square footage, other areas, etc.)				
7. Other				
B. Furniture (Compile and attach a complete list of furnishings.)				
1. Is there lounge-style, comfortable seating?				
2. Is there room for group seating?				
3. Is there room for studying?				
4. Are there any furnishings available to the individual browser or studier?				
5. Is the overall style and color scheme of the furnishings complementary to the space? (Describe.)				

Name:_____ Library:_____ Date:_____

	Yes	No	N/A	Comments
6. How many people can be simultaneously seated in the area?				
7. Other				

C. Fixtures (Compile and attach a complete list of fixtures.)

	Yes	No	N/A	Comments
1. Do signs get you to where you want to be?				
2. Is signage attractive?				
3. Is the name of the area appealing to young adults? If not, why not?				
4. Does the area have adequate shelving for				
hard covers?				
paperbacks?				
AV?				
magazines?				
5. Is there a bulletin board or display area?				
6. Are the fixtures truly functional?				
7. Is there adequate lighting?				
8. Are there any special or unique elements in the space, such as a loft, cathedral ceiling, or multiple levels?				
9. Other				

D. Collection

	Yes	No	N/A	Comments
1. Does the young adult collection consist of a variety of formats (not just books)?				
2. Is there a good selection and variety of materials?				
3. Are materials attractive looking?				

(Continued)

FIGURE 2.2 Inventory Checklist *(Continued)*

	Yes	No	N/A	Comments
4. Are materials grouped by genre or designated by a spine label (e.g., horror, science fiction)?				
5. Does the library offer "alternative" formats for young adults (videos, books on cassette and CD, music CDs, DVDs, CD-ROMs, etc.)? If so, can young adults check out these materials?				
6. Is the collection up to date?				
7. Are there young adult materials in the children's area?				
8. Are there children's materials in the young adult area?				
9. Other				
E. Display				
1. Is the collection presented in an eye-catching manner?				
2. Is there use of face-out (materials facing cover out rather than spine out) merchandising?				
3. Are new materials highlighted?				
4. Are thematic displays used?				
5. Are walls, pillars, ceilings, etc., used to their maximum display potential?				
6. Are there "point of purchase" (impulse "buying") displays used at the circulation desk?				
7. Are AV items highlighted? If not, are they in a nearby location that is attention grabbing?				

	Yes	No	N/A	Comments
8. Other				

F. Technology

	Yes	No	N/A	Comments
1. Are there any computers designated just for young adults?				
If so, how many?				
If not, where are the closest computers?				
Do computers have access to				
an online catalog?				
the Internet?				
research databases?				
games?				
word processing software?				
2. If Internet access is provided, is it filtered?				
3. Is there equipment for young adults to				
try out CD-ROMs?				
listen to books on cassette/CD?				
listen to music (stereo or listening stations)?				
4. Other				

G. Staffing

	Yes	No	N/A	Comments
1. Is it easy to discern where a young adult can find assistance?				
2. Is staff friendly and knowledgeable?				
3. Are there any staff members specifically designated to the young adult department?				
4. Is a service desk within the young adult area?				
5. Other				

Layout and Location

A floor plan is the primary tool used for analyzing layout and location. It provides a foundation for the design project, presenting a reliable overview of how things are arranged within and around the space. A floor plan allows a designer to explore options before spending time and money implementing them. An accurate floor plan will allow you to determine if you have the room to include features that you want in your new young adult space. Having the floor plan on hand throughout the inventory will prove invaluable.

For an example of a professionally rendered floor plan, refer to the Webster Public Library's plan in chapter 4. If you don't have a professionally rendered floor plan, consider making your own. See the picture of the Leominster (Massachusetts) Public Library for an example of a plan created with graph paper. Computer-assisted plans of the North Central High School Information Center (Indianapolis, Indiana) are shown for the first and second levels.

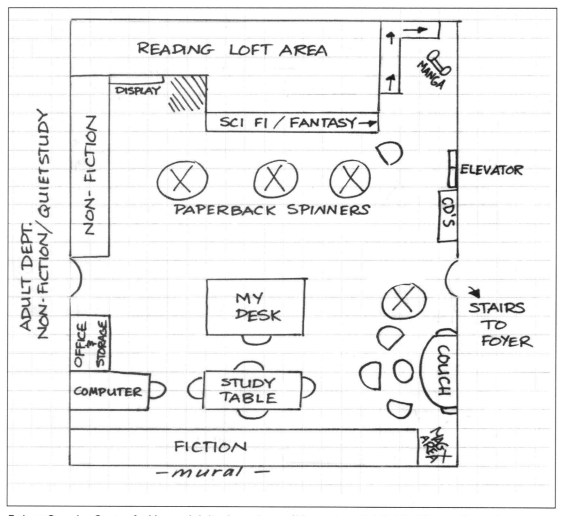

Robert Cormier Center for Young Adults, Leominster (Massachusetts) Public Library, floor plan

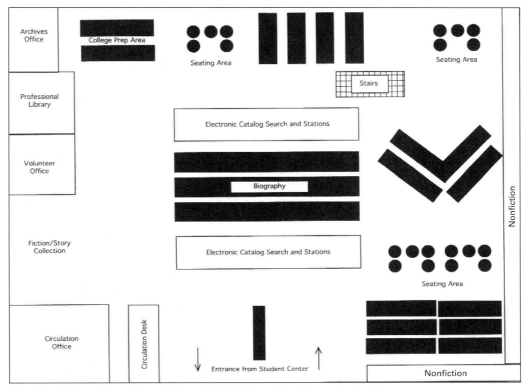

First-level floor plan of North Central High School, Indianapolis, Indiana

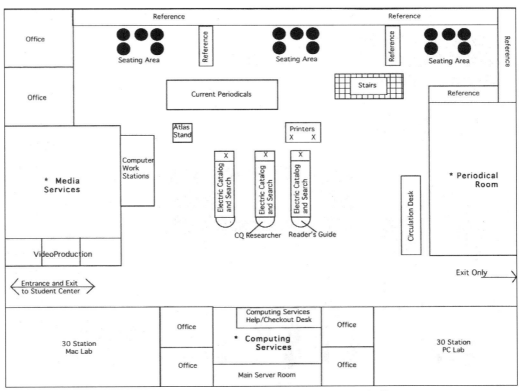

Second-level floor plan of North Central High School, Indianapolis, Indiana

Creating a Floor Plan

Be as accurate as possible when creating a floor plan. Try to keep the drawing to scale (1/4″ = 1 foot). Make all measurements in inches using a metal tape measure for accuracy.

1. Measure the wall length starting at one corner of the room and working in a clockwise direction. Draw the walls and their measurements on graph paper. Write the dimensions in one direction so you don't have to keep turning the paper to read them.

2. Measure the width of the doors as well as the distance of the doors from the ends of the walls, and draw the measurements on the graph paper.

3. Measure the width of any existing windows or other miscellaneous openings, and note it on the floor plan.

4. Include all architectural elements in the plan such as posts, pillars, lights and light switches, and hookups (telephone, computers, printers, etc.).

5. Incorporate any furniture pieces such as tables, chairs, shelving units, computer stands, etc., and make a rough sketch of their current placement in the room making sure to note their dimensions.

6. Attach any photographs of the space for additional reference.

Analyzing a Floor Plan

When analyzing your floor plan, consider the following questions:

Is the young adult area a distinctly separate space?

Where is the teen area in relationship to other departments? Where is it in relation to the entrance of the building?

What is the overall feel of the space? Is it overly crowded with no room for more materials, seating, etc.? Or maybe it is too spacious and there's ample room for materials and seating but the contents are out of proportion compared with the space itself—a warehouse feel.

How are the contents of the space arranged?

Is there any privacy and can teens be social without disturbing other patrons?

Overall, is the physical and psychological environment of the existing teen space both appropriate and appealing to teens?

How much floor space of the library is devoted to teens and how does it relate to the entire square footage of the building?

Throughout this process, keep in mind that teens are social creatures by nature, so this means don't put the young adult area next to the quiet study section or too close to the children's room. It is essential that both the location and the arrangement of the space assist in meeting adolescent needs both socially and developmentally as explained in chapter 1.

Calculating Space Needs

This is also a good time to start thinking about future square footage. The easiest way to determine the adequacy of a teen facility's square footage is to use an instrument such as Anders Dahlgren's Space Needs Worksheet found in appendix A. Dahlgren's method uses estimates for determining collection, seating, staff work, special use, and other spaces. It is best used for obtaining an approximation of a library's space needs based on its underlying service goals. Generally, this process is used for planning an entire library facility, but it can easily be adapted to young adult space planning. For a downloadable copy of the worksheet, visit the web site for the Wisconsin Department of Public Instruction. (See appendix B.)

To complete the Space Needs Worksheet, enter all relevant information based on data collected during the analysis, skipping over those sections that do not pertain to the project. Follow the guidelines as outlined on the web page because they will provide a clear understanding of the entire process. The purpose of this worksheet is to calculate square footage and to evaluate space based on collection growth and design population (i.e., the population that the expanded/improved young adult facility is expected to serve). Local school districts are an excellent resource for gathering demographic information on teens including the total number of teens in the area, population growth projection, etc.

Once the worksheet is complete, you'll be left with a thorough space analysis and an accurate representation of the gross area based on the existing facility. Depending on the size of your project, it might be helpful to go back through the steps a second time, but this time input your "projected" or "proposed" figures to get an idea of the square footage necessary for your ideal teen area. Compare your new figures with the actual square footage of the existing space. How do they measure up?

Furniture and Fixtures

Furniture, for inventory purposes, consists of the furnishings of the teen space, including tables and chairs of both the study and lounging variety. Working from your master inventory, take a look at what types of furnishings are in your library's existing teen space. Consider the following questions.

How many people can be seated simultaneously in the entire young adult area?

Is there room for group seating? For studying? For socializing?

Are there any furnishings available to the individual browser or studier such as homework carrels?

Is there lounge-style, comfortable seating?

In a young adult space, a variety of seating styles is necessary for accommodating the needs and general nature of its teenaged patrons. The overall appearance (style, color scheme, etc.) of the furnishings and how they tie in with the rest of the space is also crucial. To attract teens, it is vital to keep comfort and social needs in mind as well as the certainty that stylish, up-to-date furniture will grab their attention.

For our purposes, fixtures in a teen area primarily include shelving units, paperback spinner racks, signs, and sign holders. Other miscellaneous elements, such as lighting fixtures, pictures, and drinking fountains, could also be included here. Once again, using the master inventory as a guide, record the types of fixtures that are included in the space. Evaluate the following aspects:

Does the space have adequate shelving for hardcovers and paperbacks? (Make sure to count the total number of shelves that are currently in use.)

Are shelves empty, or are things jam-packed?

Are there display fixtures (book easels, slatwall panels, racks, etc.) in the area? What are they used for?

Is there enough room for displays and face-out merchandising at the ends of the shelves?

Are the fixtures "make do," or are they truly functional?

Is signage attractive and eye-catching?

Is there a bulletin board?

Are there any special or unique elements in the space?

Once you have thoroughly analyzed all the furnishings and fixtures, start to make a second list, dividing everything into two categories: things to throw away and things to reuse or revamp. Have this list handy throughout the remainder of the planning stages.

The Collection

A young adult materials collection may consist of books (fiction and nonfiction), graphic novels, comic books, magazines, audiovisual items (books on cassette or CD, videos, DVDs, CD-ROMs, music CDs), online databases, and games (electronic and stand alone). When initially analyzing your teen collection, refer back to the collection data gathered through your inventory and to your Space Planning Worksheet in progress. View the collection in terms of selection and variety.

Is the young adult collection strong and diverse?

What teen materials actually reside in the young adult space?

Are books the only materials in the teen area, or are other types of material incorporated?

Does the library offer alternative formats (videos, DVDs, compact discs, CD-ROMs, books on cassette, books on CD, and games) for teens?

Are there any restrictions on audiovisual materials? Can teens check out these materials?

Are young adult materials attractive and fresh?

Are items grouped by genre? If so, are genres designated by a spine label?

Is the content of the collection up-to-date?

Are there children's titles in the young adult area? Conversely, are there young adult titles in the children's collection? (If either situation exists, it may be time to talk to the children's librarian about collection development policy and, possibly, relocating age-appropriate titles.)

Display

Display refers to how the collection is presented to teens. In other words, how are the items marketed to the customer? At this point, ask:

How are teens exposed to library materials?

Is the collection presented in an eye-catching manner?

Is there use of face-out merchandising, or is everything spine out?

Are new materials highlighted?

Are thematic displays used?

Is the fiction collection broken into genres for easy browsing?

Are the walls, pillars, end panels, and ceilings used to their maximum potential?

Are there "point of purchase" displays at the reference or circulation desks? (Point of purchase means promotion of materials through interior displays, annotated booklists, window presentations, or other face-out merchandising, especially near the circulation desk, that encourage patrons to impulsively borrow an item.)

Are AV items promoted and publicized?

Do signs seem to get teens to where they want to go?

What is the "name" of the space? (Chapter 4 contains more information on naming a young adult area.)

It might be helpful at this point to start looking at local area bookstores to see how they display their items for teens. (Chapter 5 has information on this topic.) During your analysis of display, remember that an attractive, clearly labeled, and effectively merchandised area will surely pique teen interests.

Technology

Technology includes anything electronic including computers and audiovisual devices (stereos, listening stations, VCRs, DVD players, e-book readers, etc.). It also encompasses online database subscriptions, Internet access, CD-ROMs, and electronic games. When first starting a "technical inventory," begin by looking at the library's computers.

Are any PCs designated just for teens? If so, how many? If not, why, and are there any immediately adjacent to the area?

To what do these computers have access? Online catalog? The Internet? Research databases? Games?

Are there age restrictions on use of the Internet?

Is Internet access filtered for teens? If so, what is the age cutoff?

Is there restricted use of the Internet (no e-mail, no chatting, no downloading, etc.)?

Are there computers on which teens can try out CD-ROMs or listen to CDs before they check them out?

Are personal computers available with programs such as WordPerfect, Microsoft Word, Microsoft PowerPoint, Microsoft Excel, or comparable software?

Are there notebook computers that can be checked out?

Does the young adult area have earphones, listening stations, or a stereo system where teens can listen to music and books on cassette or CD?

Is a television available for teens to watch television programs or videos?

How does this information assist in planning for a more effective teen library facility? Technology is a teen magnet, and to create the ideal young adult library space, technology must be a vital part of the space plan. Because 17 million teens ages 12 through 17 use the Internet, computers with Internet access must be included in young adult areas (or in close proximity).[4] According to the Pew Internet and American Life Project, teens log on most frequently to the Internet at home. (See figure 2.3.) This makes sense in light of the many libraries that have rules restricting teens from doing many of the things they enjoy doing on the Internet; therefore, why would they want to come to the library for Internet access? We should be asking ourselves how we can create a positive environment that is conducive to constructive Internet use so teens log on at the library, rather than putting all our energies into finding reasons why the Internet is a problem. For example, figure 2.4 lists the things teens have done online. It is a great resource for generating and legitimizing ideas (Internet-related and otherwise) for a teen space plan. No matter how you look at it, a young adult space where teens can interact with their surroundings by listening to music or chatting on the Internet will keep get them in and keep them coming back for more.

FIGURE 2.3
Where Teens Log on

	Ever[1]	Most often[2]
Home	90%	83%
School	64%	11%
A friend's house	64%	3%
Library	36%	1%
Someplace else, such as at work or a cyber café	8%	1%

1. $n = 754$.
2. $n = 659$; teens who go online from multiple locations

Reproduced with permission: Pew Internet and American Life Project, Teens and Parents Survey, Nov.–Dec. 2000.

FIGURE 2.4
What Teens Have Done Online

Send or read e-mail	92%	Visit a site for their club or team	39%
Surf the web for fun	84%	Go to a web site where they can express opinions about something	38%
Visit an entertainment site	83%		
Send an instant message	74%		
Look for information on hobbies	69%	Buy something	31%
Get news	68%	Visit sites for trading or selling things	31%
Play or download a game	66%		
Research a product or service before buying it	66%	Look for health-related information	26%
Listen to music	59%	Create a web page	24%
Visit a chat room	55%	Look for information on a topic that is difficult to talk about with others	18%
Download music files	53%		
Check sports scores	47%		

Reproduced with permission: Pew Internet and American Life Project, Teens and Parents Survey, Nov.–Dec. 2000.

Staffing

By now you should have a good idea of the staffing situation in your library. Additional issues to consider during the analysis phase include the following:

> How many staff members are directly or indirectly involved with teen services?

> How many are solely dedicated to young adults?

> Is there currently a service desk within the young adult area? If not, is a service desk nearby?

> Is it easy to discern where a teenager can find assistance? (It is crucial that help be readily accessible to teens, especially since most will not seek out someone for help.)

> Are staff members friendly, approachable, and knowledgeable?

Over and over again, teens everywhere stress the importance of warm, open, and friendly people. After all, one negative experience is all it takes to turn a teenager away.

Strengths and Weaknesses

After the inventory, immediately begin classifying the elements into either a plus *or* minus category. This will provide a clear picture of what is needed to create the ideal young adult space. Dividing the inventory in this manner is an easy way to instantly organize and prioritize a wide range of elements. When proceeding through this step, remember that there are always pluses, regardless of how bleak it may seem. Figure 2.5 is a list compiled for a fictional library.

FIGURE 2.5
Strengths and Weaknesses of Library Z's Young Adult Area

Strengths	Weaknesses
Decent sized space with room for both study and casual furniture	Located in the back of the library (hidden) and next to the children's department
Located adjacent to adult/young adult non-fiction collection, college and career information, and reference department	Very little signage; boring and small signage
	No comfortable, lounge-style seating
Extensive collection of young adult paperbacks, multiple copies of popular authors and titles, and a good teen magazine collection	Books all spine out with no face-out display
	Collection needs weeding
Attractive (and potentially reusable) paperback racks	All books; audiovisual items, teen magazines, and graphic novels located in the adult area
Lots of unused wall and ceiling space	
Fiction separated into genre collections (science fiction/fantasy, mystery/horror)	

The simplest way to initiate the "plus and minus" process is to go through your inventory list and for every element ask the following questions:

Is this beneficial to the young adult area and service, or is it a hindrance?

Would this make a young adult want to hang out here? Why or why not?"

What is there about the space that could be used to attract teens? What could you get or do to make the space grab their attention?

What makes the area attractive and comfortable or ugly and unpleasant?

Can a teenager entering this library find the young adult/teen area or easily locate needed materials? Why or why not?

Are there hindrances to good service? If so, what are they? If not, what is pleasing about the services currently offered?

All data and information gathered up until this point should ultimately work to support your goals and objectives and shape your final space plan. Open communication with staff, a thorough, well thought out inventory, and as always, active teen participation will ensure that the next step of formalizing your plan and proposing it to decision makers will be a smooth and painless process.

Notes

1. Created with assistance from Renée J. Vaillancourt, "YA Assessment Outline" (Parmly Billings Library, Billings, Mont., 2000).
2. This model is based on the Junior Friends of the Library started by Nick Burke at the Union County Public Library, Lake Butler, Florida.
3. Taken in part from Dave Coleman's "Guidelines for a Successful Teen Council" as it appeared in Kimberly Hundley, "The Power of Teens: YAs Enrich San Bernardino County Library," *Today's Librarian* 3, no. 5 (May 2000): 12–15.
4. Pew Internet and American Life Project. December 2000. Available www.pewinternet.org (10 Nov. 2001).

Plan and Propose **3**

After you have a sound idea of the changes you want to make and where you're headed, concentrate on working out the details—bringing everything together into a workable plan. (In addition to using the worksheets provided in this chapter for developing your plan, consider starting a design file early in this process. For more on creating a design file, see chapter 4.) A space plan is valuable for two reasons:

It assists in organizing ideas and all related components of the project, creating a blueprint for all involved.

It is the primary tool used in presenting project information to staff, administration, and key decision makers.

A well-received space plan must be clearly thought out, flexible, and easy to understand, describing what you want to do as well as the steps you will take to get to the final product. A strong space plan will include a plan for improvement, or action steps, and quickly move on to an explanation of how the project will add value to teen services or library services on the whole. It will also contain an outline of the resources (money and people) necessary to carry out the project as well as an estimated time frame for completion. By including each of these elements, you will be left with a solid plan that is both ready to sell and ready to implement.

Action Steps

The information gathered in the inventory and analysis stage will be used as a springboard for creating a "to do" list. These action steps must be as specific as possible. Action steps serve two purposes:

1. to outline the proposed ideas in a clear, succinct manner
2. to serve as a support mechanism for goals and objectives

Appendix A has a Teen Space Planning Worksheet to record your action steps. Examples of action steps might be similar to those shown in the first column of figure 3.1. (The other columns are discussed throughout various sections in this chapter.) Throughout this process it is essential to continuously refer to your goals and objectives (discussed later in this chapter) to ensure that every action supports them and that all goals and objectives are addressed in the plan.

To determine your action steps, just think about all the things in your current teen area that you would like to add, modify, or improve. List everything you deem necessary for creating that "ideal" young adult space, from the obvious to the minuscule to the outrageous. However, be prepared to change your mind several times during the process, but don't be afraid to aim high. Everyone's ideas seem huge and out of reach at first, but with a little perseverance many of them can become a reality.

Physical Space

Two very important action steps are the determination of where the new teen area will be located and how much physical space it will occupy. The location might have a lot to do with the square footage needed to carry out the plan. (Refer to your Space Needs Worksheet from appendix A.) Intrinsic to these decisions is whether you want to relocate the teen area entirely, expand on the space you currently have, or simply improve the existing area as it stands. Regardless, remember that a successful teen area must be easily identified, easy to get to, and located near key teen-related library areas.

Making a decision on location and size will have a direct impact on the remaining action steps and will clearly announce the importance of teenagers to the library. Historically, organizations reveal what and whom they value through spatial design.[1] Even with teen demographics increasing (34 million by 2010 in the United States, alone), most libraries continue to undervalue teenagers by giving them less floor space than any other user group.[2] Therefore, take a look at the percentage of floor space the teen area currently occupies and plan to double or even triple it. Refer back to the Space Needs Worksheet to see what works best for your facility.

All action steps share one common denominator: they must all somehow relate back to the physical space of the teen area. For example, when evaluating the content of your young adult materials collection, you might want to improve the collection, weeding old materials and adding new formats. This is a great action step, but take it a step further by viewing the collection in relation to the area in which it's housed. How does the collection influence the space? How would the space improve the presentation of the collection? Another example would be the functional requirements of the area. You might decide that the focus of the area needs to be more recreational. An action step would be to incorporate comfortable seating into the teen area. Be specific about how much and what types of furnishings are to be added, always considering the space. Consider the activities that will take place in the space as well as address how the space will accommodate them.

FIGURE 3.1
Sample Space Planning Worksheet

Action Step	Value	People	Money	Time
Layout Change the floor plan to create a well-defined young adult area with a cozier and more welcoming feeling by moving four (3' x 8') shelving units.	Will give teens an identifiable space of their own Will allow them to gather and socialize without disturbing others	Professional movers Shelvers (teens and staff volunteers)	$1,000	5–8 hours
Furniture Improve the "feel" of the space by painting mural and incorporating comfortable seating Purchase one new sofa/couch and a minimum of three lounge-style chairs Relocate one additional study table with four chairs similar to existing table and chairs	Will add character and a much-needed identification of the space helping to define the variety of functions of a thriving teen area (similar to the current Children's Dept.) Will increase teen participation in library	Selectors (teens and teen librarian) Painters (teens) Movers and designers to lay out the space (teens and librarian)	$2,500	3 hours for buying trips 1.5 hours to discuss and vote 1 month to design mural and 1 week to paint it 2 hours to move and rearrange furniture
Fixtures Improve existing signage including signs that direct teens to the area and signs within the area (including paperback rack labels and genre signs) Purchase a neon look dry erase marker board for announcements Decide what to call the area and purchase a large sign to hang outside the space	Will help identify the physical space and give ownership to the teens who occupy the space Will encourage self-sufficiency in finding materials Will improve the "look" of the area and the advertisement of its goods and services Will increase teen participation in library	Designers (librarian with assistance from teens) Sign "hangers" (teens and librarian or janitor to ceiling mount hanging sign)	$300	1 hour to research 1 hour to discuss and vote at teen meeting 6–8 hours to create and hang signs
Improve use of wall space (hang posters, three-dimensional items) Install a large teen-developed and maintained bulletin board in the central portion of the space	Will increase attractiveness of space Will increase teen participation in library	Selectors (librarian and teens) "Hangers" (librarian and teens)	$75	1–2 hours
Display Increase face-out merchandising and make better use of the ends of the shelving units to help promote and highlight various materials (possibly purchase end panel display racks and easels	Will increase attractiveness and quality of collection as well as improve marketing of materials to teens for increased circulation. Will increase teen participation in library	Selectors of display units (librarian and teens) Installers (librarian and teens) Arrangers (regular responsibility of teen board members)	$150	1.5 hours to research and purchase 1 hour to arrange (reoccurring project every few weeks)

(Continued)

FIGURE 3.1
Sample Space Planning Worksheet *(Continued)*

Action Step	Value	People	Money	Time
Collection Develop young adult collection Weed hardcover and paperback teen fiction based on automated circulation report and shift collection accordingly Incorporate new formats into the area including graphic novels, manga (Japanese animation), and games Work with AV librarian to select more videos and DVDs popular with teens Relocate teen magazines from the adult section, reevaluate title selection, and establish a young adult periodical display within the teen area	Will enhance the attractiveness and teen appeal of the collection leading to increased young adult circulation for the library and increased use of the space by teens Will increase teen participation in library	Librarian to develop collection (with suggestions from teen advisors) Movers (librarian and teens)	$3,000 (reoccurring charge—suggest 20 percent increase in budget for next year)	10–15 hours
Technology Purchase three new computers and one printer Upgrade the existing young adult workstation by adding memory and installing MS Office (as used in local schools) The four new PCs will have access to the online catalog, the Internet, and research databases as purchased in conjunction with network/database librarian as appropriate for teens Allow access to the CD-ROM drive for previewing CDs	Will increase usefulness of the library to teens/students Will help encourage school/library cooperation Will improve the overall appeal of the space	Librarian and technical person to purchase and configure (possibly use a teen tech assistant to help with configuration)	$3,500	6 hours
Purchase and set-up a stereo system with a multidisc changer and extra speakers to be mounted on the walls	Will assist in creating an "atmosphere" and help draw teens to the library Will help promote use of the library to teens, getting them to hang out more frequently and at longer intervals	Purchasers (librarian and teens) Installers (teens)	$250	3 hours

Library's Mission, Goals, and Objectives

Your action steps should also describe how your ideas for the teen area mesh with your library's mission statement, goals and objectives, and long and/or short-range plans. In the simplest terms, *goals* mean "desired outcomes" and should clearly identify what you are trying to achieve. For instance, one very broad goal for this project might be: "The library will remodel its existing young adult area, creating a new, fully functional space for teens." Others might be:

"The library will build a new young adult area focusing on the recreation and academic needs of teenagers in the community" or "young adults (grades 6–12) will participate in designing and creating a new and improved young adult area for the library."

Next, move on to defining the objectives, or the way the library will measure its progress toward reaching its goals. Examples of objectives incorporating actions and measures might include the following:

Double the floor space of the existing young adult space by (date).

Hire a professional designer by (date) to consult with the young adult librarian to design a new teen area.

Train all staff in the area of customer service by (date) to deliver friendly and knowledgeable assistance to teens with homework, personal research, and recreational needs.

By (date) increase the number of items in the young adult collection by 30 percent, including adding new formats such as graphic novels, DVDs, and books on CD.

Increase technology by purchasing four new computers for the online catalog, database access, and the Internet by (date); relocate two old computers from the adult into the teen area for word processing and CD-ROM access by (date); and incorporate listening stations, a television, and a VCR/DVD player by (date).

Refer to *The New Planning for Results* by Sandra Nelson for a more in-depth look at library planning as a whole, including information on goals, objectives, and measures. For further details on establishing goals and objectives specifically for young adult services, refer to *Bare Bones Young Adult Services: Tips for Public Library Generalists* by Renée J. Vaillancourt. (See appendix B.)

A strong, well thought out teen plan takes into account young adult elements as well as considers the entire library, its functional requirements, overall vision, and inherent characteristics. Ask, "Does the library's plan coincide with the teen plan?" If so, it is imperative that you illustrate how the two work together and make a point of highlighting it in your final plan. If the two don't seem to agree ask, "How could the young adult plan be altered to better complement the library as a whole?" Don't compromise your ideals; simply try to work them into the library's plan. The more your ideas relate to the library, demonstrating an understanding of how the young adult piece fits into the entire library puzzle, the stronger the space plan will be.

Problems and Limitations

As you create your list of action steps, look for any immediately recognizable problems or limitations. It is always better to recognize potential roadblocks at the beginning rather than being unpleasantly surprised in the middle or, even worse, at the end of the process. Keep in mind the inherent characteristics of the library building itself and how they could affect your young adult action steps. For instance, you might want to build a loft in a renovated young adult area but the construction of the existing library makes it impossible, or maybe the library is located in a historical building that has specific guidelines for renovation and design. Another desired action step might be to relocate the teen area to a back corner of the library, but in the back of your mind you know that library administration and staff have expressed legitimate concerns about being able to monitor this space. This is a legitimate roadblock that you must be prepared to address. Always have an alternative to your "ideal" plan. The point here is to consider everything.

Value

Next you will need to attach meaning to your action steps and add value to your plan to help ensure your project's success. Decision makers will better realize the merit of a project if they are shown the value of your proposed ideas. The second column in figure 3.1 shows specific examples of value-added action steps.

Researching teen space projects at other libraries will also add substantial value to your plan. Begin by looking at the model teen areas featured throughout this book (as well as those that might be near you as listed in appendix C). Spaces such as these are great idea generators and confidence boosters. Perhaps there is a library near you that has recently renovated its teen area. Take a field trip—set up an appointment to visit the space and to talk to the person responsible for overseeing the project. This is one of the best steps you could take to help determine your action steps and point out their value to your plan. Any evidence you can provide that demonstrates how this type of project has been successful at other locations will encourage support in your own library. If possible, include before and after photographs from other sites as well as statistics showing increases in young adult circulation, use, and program attendance. This type of data and firsthand information provides concrete proof that teen space projects are well worth the investment. Keep in mind that you will want to concentrate on projects similar in scale to yours, but don't be afraid to present something a bit larger to "wow" your stakeholders and help illustrate your points.

Standards

During this action step and value process, take a look at how the space plan corresponds with young adult library standards for your local library system or state or national library organization. Supporting your ideas with standards such as these will add strength to your case. The Young Adult Library Services Association's (YALSA) web page is an excellent place to begin your comparison.[3] State and local standards may be more difficult to locate, and possibly nonexistent, but seek them out just the same because the resulting information could be essential in presenting your case. For instance, the New York Library Association's *Standards for Youth Services* states that every public library should have a clearly identified, separate area designated for young adults. It goes on to say that the young adult area should be physically accessible to all adolescents, easily visible and identifiable, and functional and flexible in design. It should have study tables, sufficient shelving for young adult materials, space designated for display purposes, and attractive, multipurpose furniture that is comfortable and durable. Areas for leisure reading, studying, and socializing should be included. Facilities for lighted exhibit cases, bulletin board or poster space, and computers and other technologies should be considered when the area for teenagers is designed. Magazine racks and listening stations with headphones should also be available in this area.[4] Information such as this is a valuable addition to any young adult space plan, so take the time to inquire.

Resources

To complete your library's teen space plan successfully, all aspects of the project must be considered. Those resources necessary for consideration include people, money, and time.

People

The most valuable resource of any design project is people. Whether teens, staff, volunteers, contractors, or designers, people will be responsible for carrying out the project from start to finish. Go through each action step one by one. Determine who will be responsible for each task, whether an individual or a group. Assign tasks to people immediately, so you can quickly learn where you have adequate support and where you need assistance. (See the third column in figure 3.1.) By considering this now, you leave yourself ample time to recruit volunteers if needed. However, don't worry if the assigned people and responsibilities change as the project unfolds—that is expected.

It's no secret that teens will be your biggest asset throughout the entire project. The challenge now is to decide exactly how and to what extent they will be involved. Some of you may choose to include teens throughout the entire project, and others may not. The important thing is that you *do* include them somehow. Although there are many ways to include teens in the planning stages, how will you involve them in implementing the plan? How much work will teens actually put into the project? More significantly, how much responsibility will they have in terms of money, creativity, and hands-on involvement? Look carefully at your action steps and begin thinking about assigning duties to teens based on their strengths, interests, and talents. As with anything, certain tasks may not be suitable for certain people, and this goes for teens as well as for adults. No matter how and when they are involved, teens will have the opportunity for self-expression and skill building whether they are organizing, budgeting, designing, or simply expressing their opinions, all of which will be useful to them for the rest of their lives.

> **TIP**
>
> No matter how and when they are involved, teens will have the opportunity for self-expression and skill building whether they are organizing, budgeting, designing, or simply expressing their opinions, all of which will be useful to them for the rest of their lives.

Outside Help

If the project is suddenly beginning to look too overwhelming, consider hiring a teen services consultant. According to a report of the United States Department of Education, slightly more than 10 percent of the nation's 15,000 public libraries employ a young adult specialist trained to work with teens.[5] Although this may be the case, it does not mean that public libraries are not committed to providing quality service to young adults.

If you're interested in actively pursuing young adult space development but don't have the money to hire a consultant, consider applying for a grant or asking for money in next year's budget. Two library systems that have proven successful getting grants of this nature are the Pioneer Library System (in Canandaigua, New York, see Building Big on a Small Budget later in this chapter for more details) and the San Joaquin Valley (California) Library System. The Pioneer Library System's Young Adult Services for Generalists (Library Services and Construction Act grant) and Young Adult Services Institute—Serving San Joaquin Valley Teens in the 21st Century (Library Services Technology Act grant) served to train staff in the areas of young adult service, including materials selection, programming, psychology of teens, customer service, public relations, and the public library's role in supporting the school curriculum. A major concentration of both projects was the development of teen areas and the creation of model teen spaces. Both library systems included funds to hire a consultant to carry out these duties. A sample job description for such a position might include some or all of the following:

- review the library's mission statement, long-range goals and plans
- assess existing teen library space(s) and services
- visit other young adult spaces in both newly constructed and reconfigured spaces when and if appropriate
- create young adult areas in selected model sites
- train staff to plan, create, and maintain effective and exciting young adult spaces
- instruct staff in teen collection development, programming, and marketing for teens
- develop a plan to facilitate the creation and maintenance of future young adult spaces

Constance VanSwol, Chicago Ridge (Illinois) Public Library, and Pamela Wolfanger, Marion (New York) Public Library, have both redesigned their library's teen spaces with the help of a young adult consultant. Both say that it was an invaluable investment. In fact, VanSwol reveals that the one thing that got her teen area off the ground was a $25,000 state grant. With that, Chicago Ridge was able to purchase books, shelving, and signage as well as to cover additional staff and training. To find out more about consultant services and for more information on applying for local, state, and national grants please contact your local library system or consortium, your state youth services consultant, or resources such as the American Library Association's *The Big Book of Library Grant Money 2002–2003* or its Awards, Grants, and Scholarships web page.

Budget

No matter what the size of the project, you must prepare a budget or indicate the general cost. A budget is essential in providing guidance, thus helping to better determine the overall scope of the project as well as the feasibility of the proposed ideas. This process may also assist in addressing previously overlooked details as well as help tackle big issues such as the ability to hire outside assistance such as contractors, designers, movers, etc. When putting together a budget, make it somewhat flexible because the figures being gathered are cost estimates, and at some point during the course of the project, these figures might need to be revised. (See column 4 in figure 3.1 showing cost estimates. Note that these figures are for illustrative purposes only.)

When drafting your project budget, take a look at the figures collected in chapter 2, comparing the existing young adult budget with the overall library budget and other departments of the library. It is important that you include all budgetary findings in your final proposal, being careful to point out your awareness of the overall library budget and how your project can effectively and affordably fit with that budget. How do they measure up? Is there any flexibility in your existing young adult budget? Could you apply any of your regular budget to project costs? Are there any "hidden" or unused monies in the overall library budget that you might be able to use (such as capital improvement funds)? Investigate any budget information available from comparable projects. For example, has the young adult area in your library ever gone through a redesign or renovation? If so, how long ago did it occur, and how much did it cost? Have any other departments in your library gone through a similar project? If so, how much was spent? Take a look at design projects at other libraries in your state and out of state. Try to find projects similar in scale so the costs are comparable.

Producing a detailed budget proposal will be a key element in gaining support and persuading administration that its money will be invested well. No matter what size project, if a budget has not been outlined, don't wait for someone to tell you what you have to spend. Go ahead and start preparing a budget of your own. Your initiative and organization might just influence administration decisions.

Estimates

Undoubtedly, your level of involvement with finances will be entirely based on the size of your project. With small-scale ventures, where only a few hundred dollars are involved, you might be able to use existing library funds or outside donations. With a larger scale project, such as a renovation or expansion, more extensive budget work is required. In this latter situation, is your project large enough that it will go out to bid? With larger projects it is also quite common for budgetary guidelines to be predetermined by administration. If so, you may have to fight for the funds necessary to create the space you want.

You will find that written estimates are essential when estimating costs for a budget. Most organizations have procedures for collecting and comparing estimates. For example, the procedure might state that for items or services over $500, a minimum of three quotations must be collected. No matter what the rule is at your library, it is important that you follow its guidelines. At the same time, keep in mind that it never hurts to gather multiple estimates for everything. Because you will be able to compare and contrast information from multiple sources, you will get a better understanding of what you are looking for and, ultimately, end up with a more accurate proposed budget.

When gathering estimates for each item or service, choose one vendor to deal with for the initial quotation. Draft the request with as much detail as possible. Once the vendor returns the estimate, look it over to make sure that it is accurate and that it includes exactly what you're asking for. Don't be afraid to make modifications or to send it back for clarification. When the estimate is finalized, use it as a model to draft requests to two or three more vendors. This way each vendor receives the same request so you can compare apples to apples. When at all possible, try to avoid gathering quotations by telephone because there is a greater chance for miscommunication and confusion. Get everything in writing, perhaps through e-mail or fax. Attach copies of the estimates to your budget worksheet for easy reference.

Action Step Budget The best way to begin estimating project expenses is to determine the cost of each item outlined in the action steps of your space plan. Figure 3.2 shows a sample action step budget. Please note that this budget does not take into account all action steps shown in figure 3.1. Four action steps were chosen to give you a basic idea of how to complete the chart. When completing *your* action step budget, make sure that you include all action steps and that everything adds up to 100 percent. (For your convenience, an Action Step Budget Worksheet is provided in appendix A.) The notes section should include information such as the company that provided the estimate and specifics of what was quoted, etc. Attach written estimates and any informational notes. As you proceed through your own budget worksheet, categorize each action step, breaking each out into as much detail as possible and gathering estimates for each item listed. Your action steps will take on a new form— moving from a narrative description to a more detailed listing.

Categorized Budget A good budget will include all anticipated expenditures. In addition to basic materials expenses (furnishings, fixtures, computers, collection materials, etc.), your budget may also include estimates for the following items:

> professionally rendered drawings or plans
>
> in-house personnel costs, for example, additional staff hours to help move materials and furnishings
>
> consultant fees or miscellaneous outside labor charges (professional design services, movers, painters, and contractors)
>
> rental equipment (stack movers, extra book carts, carpet cleaner, and painting gear)
>
> wiring (cost of additional or new electrical outlets, network drops, and telephone lines)
>
> insurance coverage (for large-scale projects and for volunteers who will be moving books and heavy items)
>
> reoccurring charges such as telecommunications fees and software upgrades

FIGURE 3.2
Action Step Budget

Action Step	Current Budget	Proposed Project Budget	Difference	Percent of Project Budget (Difference/ Total)	Notes
Layout Change the floor plan to create a well-defined young adult area with a cozier and more welcoming feeling by moving four (3′ x 8′) shelving units.	NA	$1,000	$1,000	14.7%	Includes the cost outlines by Company A. Personnel to move and reinstall shelving units. (No charge for labor and supplies to move books from old shelves— all done by teen volunteers.)
Furniture Improve the "feel" of the space by painting and incorporating comfortable seating Purchase one new sofa/couch and a minimum of three lounge-style chairs Relocate one additional study table with four chairs similar to existing table and chairs	NA	$2,500	$2,500	36.8%	Estimates noted were received from companies B and C. See attached estimates for more details.
Fixtures Improve existing signage including signs that direct teens to the area and signs within the area (including paperback rack labels and genre signs) Purchase a neon look dry erase marker board for announcements Decide what to call the area and purchase a large sign to hang outside the space	NA	$ 300	$ 300	4.4%	Directional signs as specified by company D and neon marker order from company E. The teen advisory group is looking into fundraising ideas to raise money for large sign to hang outside the space.
Technology Purchase 3 new computers and one printer Upgrade the existing young adult workstation by adding memory and installing MS Office (as used in local schools). The four new PCs will have access to the online catalog, the Internet, and research databases as purchased in conjunction with network/database librarian as appropriate for teens Allow access to the CD-ROM drive for previewing CDs	$500	$3,500	$ 3,000	44.1%	Computers to be purchased on contract #12345 from company F. Memory and software to be purchased from company G (academic pricing on software). All databases and Internet are to be purchased by network librarian through annual budget.
Total	**$500**	**$7,300**	**$ 6,800**	**100%**	

long-term young adult budget adjustments (for example, additional funds necessary for maintaining new collections, increasing programming, and adding staff)

packing materials (boxes and labeling materials may be necessary if you are planning an extensive move where storage is involved)

publicity

Once all the potential expenses have been outlined, start prioritizing the budget items, listing items in order of their importance or significance to the project. What absolutely has to be done first? Can anything wait? (Can you divide the project into phases so it's not so monetarily overwhelming?) Can anything be revised to better fit the budget? Is there anything on the list that you absolutely cannot afford? If so, what are the alternatives? Can something be scaled down, or is outside funding for big-ticket items an option? Highlight items on the list that require an alternative funding source and make note of whom to contact.

To help illustrate the financial projections, calculate budget percentages for each action item. This will show what part of the budget will be directed to each item on your list. It might also be helpful to divide the project into general budget categories, such as furniture/fixtures, consultant fees, and materials, so you can see how the funds are being allocated. Figure 3.3 is an example of a categorized budget used to determine what funding will be needed for a project. The difference column in particular provides a total budget figure based on the difference between the current and proposed budgets. The percent column shows exactly where the money is going and how the expenses are divided. This column may also prove helpful during your presentation, so be prepared to provide explanations regarding distribution of funds (i.e., why more money is being spent on one category over another). (See appendix A for a Categorized Budget Worksheet.) You may also find you need to adjust some of your figures because sometimes the categories come out much different than anticipated. Once your figures have been firmed up, consider creating a graph using the numbers from the category worksheet. (See figure 3.4.) Keep in mind that illustrations such as graphs add a nice touch to a final presentation by adding variety and color as well as a way to present numbers clearly.

Building Big on a Small Budget

If library funds are limited, don't be discouraged. If you are smart about it, you can create an absolutely wonderful teen space on a small or even nonexistent budget. Before putting together your proposal, make sure you have tapped all potential resources. Consider all funding sources as well as free materials or resources from the community and within your own library. For example, Laura Gruniger, young adult librarian for the Mercer County Library System in Lawrenceville, New Jersey, revealed that most of the big-ticket items in her teen space were already in place elsewhere in the library. (See chapter 4 for more information on what Laura and other librarians have found for free.)

Another way to help reduce initial costs is to consider dividing the project into phases. In this way you can distribute the cost over a two-year period. (Refer to the schedule section later in this chapter.)

FIGURE 3.3
Categorized Budget

Category	A. Current Budget	B. Proposed Project Budget	C. Additional Funds Needed to Complete Project (B – A)	D. Percent of Project Budget (C/Total C)
Architect/designer and consultant fees	NA	$ 1,500	$ 1,500	10.7%
Furniture and fixtures	NA	$ 3,000	$ 3,000	21.4%
Labor (remodeling, moving, etc.)	NA	$ 1,000	$ 1,000	7.1%
Supplies	$ 300	$ 500	$ 200	1.4%
Rental equipment	NA	NA	NA	0.0%
Technology	$ 1,500	$ 3,750	$ 2,250	16.0%
Collection development	$ 9,000	$13,800	$ 4,800	34.2%
Misc. long-term expenses (i.e., additional staffing, telecommunications costs for Internet access)	NA	$ 1,000	$ 1,000	7.1%
Publicity	$ 200	$ 500	$ 300	2.1%
Total	**$11,000**	**$25,050**	**$14,050**	

FIGURE 3.4
Budget Categories by Percentage

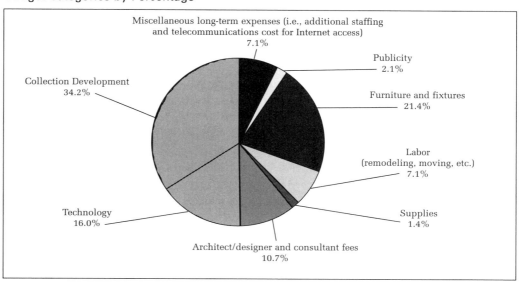

If you are still not convinced that you can renovate a teen area on a small budget, take a look at the Pioneer Library System in Upstate New York. In 1996, the system was awarded a grant to fund Young Adult Services for Generalists. This project enabled four small rural libraries (serving populations under 11,000) to develop their young adult services and redesign their teen spaces.[6] Each library was given $1,200 for collection development, $370 for programming, $190 for promotional materials, and a modest $600 budget for space redesign expenses. You would be amazed at what they accomplished for only $600. For example, with good planning, a little paint, some new modern shelving, and a lot of teen volunteer hours, the Phelps (New York) Community Memorial Library, a member of the Pioneer Library System, transformed a once dismal young adult space into a vibrant, active teen center. (In fact, within the first six months, young adult circulation increased over 300 percent.) (Chapter 4 has more details on the Phelps Community Memorial Library.)

Raising Funds

Alternative financial sources may include Friends of the Library (adult and young adult groups), a library foundation, grants, private donations, and corporate sponsorship. A staff brainstorming session may produce additional ideas for fund sources. For example, Sue Knesel at the Campbell County Library in Gillette, Wyoming, has had great luck funding her young adult area with something in her community called the One Cent Fund. The fund is composed of tax monies that are levied every four years. Her community can use it for whatever projects it wishes, and one of its highest priorities is for programs for youth. When Knesel submits her county budget each year, she asks for One Cent money for young adult-related items such as materials, furniture, and computers. Each year she has received $500 toward programs and about $3,000 toward materials. This is all above and beyond her regular budget; however, the first year she had a teen department it represented her entire budget.

Another example comes from the Marion Public Library in Marion, New York. The library obtained corporate sponsorship and a donation of $5,000 from a local food processing company to design and furnish the library's new teen area. (The area is described in chapter 4.) Although this sponsor did not seem like a typical donor for a teen facility, library manager Pamela Wolfanger said, "They (Seneca Foods) wanted to give money for the children's area, and since I already had a donor for the children's room, I took the opportunity to promote teens. I explained how the library tends to 'lose' kids after sixth grade and that I wanted to do something for this age group that would keep them around. I simply stated that teens are every bit as important as toddlers, and they agreed."

Marion Public is a small library that serves less than 5,000 people, so this was a considerable donation for them. For the overall building project, the library also received a $24,500 construction grant from the State of New York and $15,000 from legislators. Although these additional funds were designated for the entire building project, they serve as examples of the potential funding resources available. When trying to obtain financial support from outside sources, Wolfanger is emphatic about being a cheerleader for your cause. "If you believe in your project, you have to make others believe in it too," she says. "Never be afraid to ask."

Teens can also be instrumental in raising money for their teen space in the library. Following are a few examples of how teens have been involved:

The teen board at the Campbell County Public Library in Gillette, Wyoming, went to work to raise money for a TV, VCR, and CD player for their teen room. They sold soda and chips at a library-sponsored Teen Bands in the Park program.

Tricia Segal's young adult advisory board at the Fort Vancouver Regional Library in Vancouver, Washington, helped write a grant to get furniture for the new teen area being moved from a mall library to a new store-front location. The group also held a book sale and fundraiser under the auspices of the adult Friends group to raise money for the teen summer reading program. The library's foundation agreed to match up to $5,000 of the money raised by the group to help pay for incentives.

The young adult board in the Laramie County Library System, in Cheyenne, Wyoming, raised funds for furnishings by helping out at their library foundation's book sale. They negotiated 3 percent of the overall take. YA services manager Amelia Shelley said she would push for 5 percent next time. Shelley's group has also sold tie-dyed T-shirts with their young adult logo on them—Reading Road Trip. The board did the tie-dyeing, and the circulation staff sold the shirts. They made $800 altogether ($10 profit per shirt). The shirts were such a big hit that a long sleeved version is in the wings, and the library board agreed to match up to $750 of their funds. This means the young adult board can look into purchasing new furniture.

Time

It is always wise to think of your plan in terms of time. Devising a schedule can help make your project more manageable by assigning reasonable time allotments to each task to be completed. Begin creating a timetable by going back to your Space Planning Worksheet and arranging the action steps in the order that they need to occur, prioritizing your plan. Next, jot down a general time estimate for each event sequenced, determining how long each item will take to complete. (See column 5 of figure 3.1 for an example of time estimates.) Some tasks may take days. Others may take weeks, months, or even years depending on budget, project size, and staffing. When assigning deadlines and time frames to activities, be sure to take into consideration the people you've previously assigned to perform those duties. As with everything else in this project, be realistic, but don't be afraid to aim high and set goals for yourself, the project, and the people who are participating.

Once a schedule has been devised, add everything together to get an overall estimate for completion of the project. Some design projects might be carried out within months, but others might take a year or two before they are finished. After overseeing a 750-square-foot teen space renovation for the Schaumburg Township District Library in Schaumburg, Illinois, teen coordinator Amy Alessio says that a clear project time line (and deadline) is crucial, especially when using an outside designer. Because her library hired a design company for its teen center and the company was in great demand, the library had to wait almost a year for the project to be completed.

If it is not feasible for the project to be completed all at once, perhaps the action steps could be divided into phases. This may be especially useful for small-budget, long-term (i.e., those that will occur over the course of a year or more), or large-scale projects. If the project is of significant size, consider using a software program, such as Microsoft Project, to help prepare your schedule and keep you on target. No matter what size your project, once the timetable has been devised, it is essential that you try to adhere to it as much as possible, but be realistic—updating and revising are allowed.

Presenting the Proposal

Before making any formal presentations, look over all your findings and ideas. Make certain you are familiar with every part of the plan and can enthusiastically discuss any questions that arise. Take a look at your original goals and objectives, double-checking that they are clearly represented and defined in the space plan. If you discover any last-minute gaps in your plan, fill them in, even if they seem nominal. Never go into a proposal unprepared or with an incomplete plan or you will find yourself with a quickly fading project. You are the authority on this topic, so be prepared and be confident. If you are sincere and passionate about the project, it will show in the presentation. However, no matter how much you prepare, it is always possible that someone may touch upon a topic for which you don't have the answers. If this happens, be honest. Say that you'll have to look into it and get back with an answer.

Any worthwhile young adult space presentation should include handout copies of the space planning worksheet, action step and categorized budget worksheets, graphs, and any other key materials you deem worthy of presenting. Be wary of handing out too much paperwork. Focus on a few essential items. The rest of the plan can be presented using flip charts, posters, a computer presentation (such as Microsoft PowerPoint), or any other creative method you want. You might also consider incorporating and highlighting the following items somewhere in your presentation:

- supportive comments and quotations about the project from staff, teens, and teachers
- interesting ideas generated from staff brainstorming sessions, teen advisory meetings, or focus groups
- two or three of the most exciting or innovative action steps items with sample drawings, photos, clippings from catalogs, or quotations
- the results (both statistically and photographically) of comparable projects from other libraries

Use presentation boards to help illustrate ideas and provide inspiration. (For more information on presentation boards, see Creating a Design File in chapter 4.) The most successful sales pitches always have that visual "wow" factor. Ideas must be sold, and seeing is believing.

Regardless of how great your plan and proposal are, you must always be prepared for rejection. It's an unfortunate reality, but not all plans are approved (at least not right away). So, what do you do if the initial plan is rejected? Do you go back to the drawing board and start from scratch? Of course not. Simply make the necessary alterations—whether that means scaling down the project a bit, revising the budget, or doing more research. When you are satisfied with the changes, go back and present it again. It never hurts to ask those reviewing your proposal to give you feedback for future reference. Don't give up, and don't get discouraged.

Spend time creating a space plan equipped with a clearly outlined, value-added strategy for improving the space consisting of careful allocation of resources including money, people, and time. Stepping into a presentation with this quantity and quality of information along with a few "added extras" will surely impress decision makers and start the wheels turning. More importantly, you will reap the benefits of all your hard work when you begin the design and decorating phase.

Notes

1. Anthony Bernier, "On My Mind: Young Adult Spaces," *American Libraries* 29, no. 9 (Oct. 1998): 52.

2. Peter Zollo, *Wise Up to Teens: Insight into Marketing and Advertising to Teenagers* (Ithaca, N.Y.: New Strategist, 1999): 20.

3. See www.ala.org/yalsa/yalsainfo/competencies.html.

4. New York Library Assn. Youth Services Section, *The Key to the Future: Revised Minimum Standards for Youth Services in Public Libraries of New York State* (New York: New York Library Assn. Youth Services Section, 1994), 27–34.

5. Regina Minudri and Francisca Goldsmith, "The Top Ten Things You Need to Know about Teens," *School Library Journal* 45, no. 1 (Jan. 1999): 30–1.

6. A Young Adult Services for Generalists Grant was awarded to the Pioneer Library System in 1996. The project included four Upstate New York public libraries: the Phelps Community Memorial Library, Dansville Public Library, Lyons Public Library, and the Stevens Memorial Library.

4 Design and Decorate

Now that the plan is in order, avoid the temptation to go right out and start shopping. With the endless choices in today's marketplace, jumping head first into a furniture or paint store without preparation can be both intimidating and frustrating. Before you make any purchases, it is essential to figure out what you need as well as what decorating items you want. Whether doing it yourself or with the assistance of a professional designer, begin by finding an inspiration, move on to developing the style and character of the space, and then start experimenting with the layout and the décor.

Working with Architects and Designers

At this point, you should have determined whether the project will be done in-house or with the assistance of a professional architect or designer or a combination. When working with an architect or designer, communicate effectively and record the date and minutes of meetings. In addition to those items outlined on your Teen Space Planning Worksheet, consider or include the following:

> the importance of sound and light including access to, control of, and amount of it
>
> computing and print research facilities
>
> study and classroom areas
>
> open spaces to encourage supervision and communication
>
> flexiblility
>
> growth[1]

Furthermore, pay careful attention to the following elements:

> *Acoustics* If noise is an issue, plan on installing elements to reduce sound such as carpeting, baffles in the ceiling, and interior barriers such as low walls constructed within the space, strategic placement of bookcases, and other large fixtures.

Climate Control   If you are in a school or large public library, consider separate climate controls for heat and air. Place return air vents high on walls or in the ceiling to allow for maximum wall space for shelving.

Windows and Doors   To allow for maximum installation of wall-mounted shelving, windows should occupy a minimum of the wall space. Doors should be light enough to be opened by teens. Avoid having thresholds that teens and staff may trip over.

Electric, Data, and Telephone   Include ample electrical and data outlets throughout. Locate wall-mounted outlets where they are easily accessible (i.e., not within the shelving). Install floor outlets for instructional, listening, and viewing areas. Locate electrical outlets (each with a dedicated circuit if possible) at all computer workstations. Integrate phone jacks, wiring for cable television, etc., where appropriate. If appropriate for your space, install necessary wiring for ceiling-mounted projection and video surveillance.

Security System   If a security system is important, protect computers by locating the security system away from them. Better security can also be achieved by positioning high-demand materials near service areas or creating good sight lines to the teen area.

Storage   Plan for adequate space and equipment for storage in staff areas and in the teen area proper.[2]

In addition, the following discussion about working with interior designers also applies to working with architects.

If you are not using an architect to plan a new building or addition, you may want the assistance of an interior designer. The primary role of an interior designer is to create a total creative solution for an existing space from conceptual planning to aesthetics to technical solutions. A designer works with a client to achieve a desired result based on several factors including the people who will occupy the area and the space's intended functions. A good designer will immediately inquire about each of these things as well as discuss practical considerations such as color, lighting, acoustics, furnishings, accessories, floor coverings, and potential limitations or anticipated problems with the space.

When searching for professional assistance, always interview multiple designers or firms. Look for someone who specializes in government or institutional design. Although you are not limited solely to this type of design company, they are the ones who are the most familiar with the needs and requirements of libraries. If you are prepared and organized and can communicate clearly, you'll be well on your way to finding a successful design partner.

During the interview process be prepared to answer and discuss the following types of questions:

- For whom is the space being designed?
- What activities will take place there?
- What is the time frame?
- What is the budget?
- What is the square footage to be designed?

- Is this a remodeling project or a new construction?
- What is the desired image or meaning of the finished project?[3]

Throughout the interview, keep in mind that you are looking for someone you feel comfortable with, who is willing and eager to listen to your ideas, and most importantly, who is enthusiastic about incorporating the features that you and your teen advisors want. Those who have worked with professional designers feel that a truly good designer is one who incorporates the library's ideas into theirs and enthusiastically involves the teens from the beginning. Such cooperation really adds to the teen appeal of the space.

If you are interested in hiring a designer but are hindered by a limited budget, consider hiring a Young Adult Consultant who specializes in making over teen spaces. Another idea is to ask a design company if you can purchase the initial concepts or drawings and then find the furniture and accessories on your own and do the decorating yourself.[4] Yet another option is to consider looking for a designer who will provide consultation on an hourly or daily basis instead of for the duration of the project. Any of these options would save a significant amount of time and money.

TIP

Those who have worked with professional designers feel that a truly good designer is one who incorporates the library's ideas into theirs and enthusiastically involves the teens from the beginning.

No matter who you end up working with, always practice the three *C*s of communication—be clear, concise, and consistent. Don't expect a designer or consultant to read your mind. Be prepared to ask lots of questions and to take notes as well as to present samples of items and ideas from pictures, photos, and drawings. The more you put the three *C*s into practice, the better the designer will be at understanding and interpreting your ideas into a final design plan. To further develop a successful working relationship with a designer or consultant, keep the following procedures in mind:

Define your priorities and convey your expectations.

Understand the scope of the agreement.

Share your expertise in a positive way.

Review codes, ADA requirements, etc., before the project gets too far along to avoid disappointments if an idea doesn't meet requirements.

Educate yourself in the language of design, architecture, engineering, and technology.

Develop a relationship of trust and respect.

Remember that professional consultants or designers are compensated based on their time, so use that time wisely.

Communicate, communicate, communicate.

Getting Inspired

A successful design begins with a flash of inspiration. Inspiration is an integral part of design; it sparks creativity and imbues teen spaces with personality and teen appeal. Inspiration could come from one's background, surroundings, or personal interests. In fact, the best inspiration for a new young adult space will likely come from teens themselves. However, before scheduling any meetings with teens, consider devising one or two ideas of your own just to get thought processes started. Get inspiration from those places teens like to be, draw a comparison between those places and the library, and then begin to formulate a design plan that incorporates what you've observed.

Teen Environments

Now more than ever, it is imperative that you become familiar with the places and things most important to teens. Just as you discovered a lot about teens by seeing what was in their lockers (figure 1.3), taking a look at a teenager's bedroom can also help you understand what they are like. When the members of the *Teen Spaces* teen advisory council were asked where they most like to hang out, their first response was their bedroom. Examine this response carefully because it will provide some of the best pointers on the subject of teens, their tastes, likes, and dislikes. In fact, close observation of teen bedrooms tells us how they sit, study, and relax and what recreations they like and what they read.[5]

Teens like the comfort and softness of their beds and pillows and the warm, relaxed atmosphere that allows them to listen to music or eat a snack when studying. Designing a young adult space in a library without taking these elements into account would be foolish because part of being inspired means coming to grips with what teens like—not necessarily what adults like. It means looking for alternatives, being creative, and resisting the temptation to go with what you've always done—"traditional" library furnishings, ideas, and policies. It's all about searching for something a little different and making teens feel at home. A good teen-inspired design includes a place for them to study comfortably as well as an area for them to hang out and do the things they like to do (talk, listen to music, and have fun).

After studying the places where teens hang out, solidify your teen perspective by browsing through teen magazines, retail catalogs geared toward adolescents, and young adult-related web sites. (See appendix B.) Also take a look at a few general decorating and design resources such as television design shows and decorating-related web sites, books, and magazines. This will give you the much-needed "design" perspective and a basic understanding of decorating principles, materials, and concepts. (Appendix B also includes lists of such resources.)

Once you have one or two ideas in mind, immediately discuss them and any potential concerns with your director. Talk about how the teen area will coordinate with the rest of the library. Ask if it is acceptable for the teen space to differ from the main library in style and décor. Find out specifically how much it can or cannot deviate from the rest of the library. Be very clear about what determines when a decorating scheme or design idea has surpassed what is permissible by your standards and the administration's standards. Once everyone is in agreement regarding the "rules" and boundaries, get teens involved as soon as possible.

TIP

Include teens in design workshops or focus groups.

Teen Design Groups

Include teens in design workshops or focus groups. (See chapter 1 for recruitment ideas.) To make this group really successful, try to get at least ten teens involved (ideally, anywhere from ten to thirty participants). Include a variety of ages, both library users and nonusers, and males and females. Whenever possible, divide into small work teams. Assign teams different tasks, and ask them to present their findings to the group. For consistency and fairness, let them know they must be willing to participate for the duration of the project. If you grab their attention and intrigue them at the first meeting, you won't have any problem getting them to come back.

When you've gathered a teen group, schedule meetings on the same day of the week and at the same time every few weeks or as the project time line dictates. Present a general written agenda for each session. Review the tasks at hand, presenting any ideas that have transpired since the previous meeting, and then open up the floor to discussion. Depending on the size of the group and the topic, allow 15 to 30 minutes for brainstorming. Because it's crucial to keep good records, assign one member to record the minutes of the meeting and another member to list the ideas from the brainstorming session on a board or large pad at the front of the room.

Following are a few ideas to help plan the meeting agendas.[6] (Depending on the size of the group and scope of the project, you might want to divide these meetings into multiple sessions.)

MEETING 1: Introduction and Ground Rules

Explain the purpose and scope of the project, and ask teens what they would like to see in the library that would make them and their friends visit the library regularly. Begin to discuss the location of the new space and any other immediate concerns. This meeting is crucial because it is your first chance to let teens know that they are a vital part of the project and that you want them to freely express their ideas. Lay the ground rules of the project so participants are clear about the limitations before moving ahead. Without a doubt, it will be easier to present rules at the onset rather than have to veto ideas once everyone is excited. At the end of the meeting, consider asking participants to create a collage of their ideas. Collages would consist of pictures from magazines or the web that illustrate their ideas. Have them bring their work back to the next meeting.

MEETINGS 2 and 3: Inspirations and Thematic Ideas

Share inspirational resources with teens, keeping in mind that most items such as decorating books and shows on Home and Garden television may be unfamiliar to many teenagers. Consider taping a series of decorating programs to present at the meeting. The point here is to expose teens to a variety of resources to inspire them and give them options. Present a few of your own ideas, and ask for opinions. Once everyone has brainstormed, vote on a favorite theme. (See the following section on themes.)

MEETINGS 4–7: Decorating

Use these meetings as springboards for discussion of potential color schemes, furnishings, layout, and accessories that will complement the theme of the space. Limit discussion to one or two topics per meeting. Show samples or photos

TIP

At the end of the meeting, consider asking participants to create a collage of their ideas.

of furnishings, paint, material, accessories, and so forth, and have teens vote on what they like best. (See the decorating section later in this chapter.) If you are working with a professional designer, have him or her visit the group, present ideas, and show samples. Planning "buying trips" would be another welcomed component of these sessions.

TIP

Let teens decide what materials are to be included in their new space.

Meeting 8: The Final Design

Present and discuss the final floor plan, renderings, models, furniture samples, etc. This would also be a good time to discuss the name of the new area. (See the naming and signage section at the end of this chapter.)

Meetings 9–   : Collection Development

Let teens decide what materials are to be included in their new space—graphic novels, magazines, music, etc. (Refer to chapter 5 for more ideas on this topic.)

Developing a Theme

A theme is a main idea that provides focus for a space by eliminating choices that won't fit. Themes can be direct or subtle, serious or whimsical. Whatever it is, it will say something about the people for whom the space is designed. Once a theme is selected, it will be easier to determine the remaining components of the space because selections will be made based on that which would best illustrate the main idea.

The possibilities for themes for a teen area are endless and limited only by your imagination. However, there is one small caution—try to stay away from trendy themes that involve permanent or costly items. Keep in mind that "trendy" means quickly outdated, and although it is important to choose something that teens will like and enjoy, it is equally important to work with an idea that will endure the test of time (or at least last until you can afford to revamp the teen area again). Trendy ideas and elements are definitely a double-edged sword because it's no secret that "trendy" attracts most teens. Therefore, don't disregard that which is "all the rage," instead, turn it around and think of ways to mix practical with trendy.

Be prepared for the theme of your teen area to be influenced by the overall theme of the library facility. With any luck, you will have a designer or an administration that feels that a teen area should speak for itself and not be shaped by the other areas of the library. Of course this is an ideal scenario. Realistically, this is not always the case. Many times a library may have specific guidelines for renovation or interior decoration, and these rules are generally in place for good reason. For instance, the library may lease space in a building of historical significance, and part of the lease may stipulate rules for interior decoration and renovation. If this is the situation, get creative and come up with ways to tie in the desired teen theme with the existing space.

For example, the Phelps (New York) Community Memorial Library teen area was renovated in 1996 as part of the Pioneer Library System's Adult Services for Generalists project funded by an LSCA grant. The budget for this redesign was

Phelps (New York) Community Memorial Library teen area before renovation

Same view of the Phelps teen area after renovation

a meager $600. It was a space that housed modern furnishings and a brightly colored mural in a library that was once a church. Administrators were initially hesitant about the "modern" approach, but because the teen area was located in its own separate room and the design and concept of the mural were so well thought out, the board decided that it did not disrupt the rest of the library. In fact, when the colors of the mural in the teen area were tied in with the colors in the building's stained glass windows, it provided quite a dramatic and appealing result. As shown in the first photo, the area was an unused storeroom in the library. (The computers were ready to be recycled.) The second photo shows the area after renovation with butterfly chairs, a mural painted by local teens, and lots of new materials. The area also contains grid shelving and a comfy ottoman that can be moved around the room. The finished space is an inviting space for teens to hang out.

As another example, the Swampscott (Massachusetts) Public Library has also done a fantastic job working around its library surroundings. Its teen area is all about ownership, personalization, interest, uniqueness, and creativity. Hanging CDs and a teens banner denote the space. Four roly rockers invite teens to browse and hang out. Posters are hung everywhere, and materials are displayed throughout the area—on shelves, tables and even windowsills. Old tables and a paperback rack were rescued and rejuvenated with some brightly colored paint. A listening center rounds out the space.

Potential themes for teen spaces are everywhere. Just take a look at what's going on in the world and what's popular. When selecting a theme, members of the *Teen Spaces* advisory council caution adults about choosing themes and related décor that are either too adult or too juvenile. They also recommend picking something that will be popular with both males and females. Therefore, it is essential that you involve teens in this entire process because you might think you have the best idea in the world for a young adult area but teenagers might have a totally different opinion.

Swampscott (Massachusetts) Public Library's teen area

The themes presented in the following sections can be adapted and applied to libraries and budgets of all types and sizes. They may be expanded or simplified based on your setting and circumstances. Look at the ideas, glean what you can, and apply the elements you like to your particular situation. Use these themes to spark your imagination and the imagination of the teens helping you.

Art Theme

With an art theme you may want to select from one or more art periods or styles including modern art, Italy and the Renaissance, Impressionism, art deco, or others. You could have teens emulate their favorite artists' styles and create their own masterpieces in a variety of mediums (paint, sculpture, etc.).

City or Metropolitan Theme

Considering a metropolitan theme, here are some ideas developed by the *Teen Spaces* advisory council:

> Cut out shapes of buildings using large boards or pieces of foam core and decorate them with paint. Cut holes to make windows, and insert Christmas tree lights from behind. Make sure there is easy access to an electrical outlet before mounting the "buildings" on the walls. Also, consider using a power strip so the lights can easily be turned on and off. Paint

the ceiling to look like a sky, and strategically affix glow-in-the-dark star stickers or use fluorescent paint. (Note that there are probably not too many times when the lights should be off in this area.)

Incorporate a variety of modern furnishings including overstuffed couches, butterfly chairs, and industrial looking tables and accessories.

Use inlaid carpet to mimic grass, sidewalks, and roads.

Create a room within a room by designing separate areas for studying, socializing, etc.

Include a scaled-down mockup of a subway car along one of the walls of the area. Find a photo to use as a model. Hang subway handles from the ceiling and insert silver metal poles strategically.

Coffeehouse Theme

In 2001, the Marion Public Library was a one-room storefront library located in rural Upstate New York. The teen space went from one bookcase in the old facility to an entire corner (99 square feet) of the new library. It has a café-like theme with snack tables, an "open" sign, and coffeehouse poetry on the walls. A resident artist who was inspired by poetry written in a local ninth grade English class painted the mural.

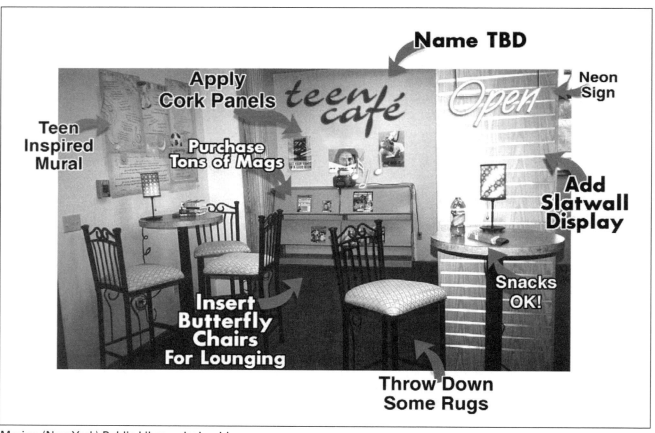

Marion (New York) Public Library design ideas

Marion Public Library mural inspired by local teen poets

Culture Theme

The theme could center around a multicultural or single culture focus. It might include a mural depicting life and images from around the world as shown in the previous photos of the Phelps Community Library.

High-Tech Theme

A high-tech theme might incorporate metal furnishings, rope lighting, touches of silver and black, and an overall minimalist look to create a futuristic feel.

History Theme

For a history theme, go back in time. Generally the 1950s, 60s, 70s, and 80s are most popular with teens right now. You could even combine all those decades with each surface (walls, floor, and ceiling) representing a different time.

Hollywood Theme

Who's hot and who's not? What's in and what's out? You'll find out soon enough if this is the theme of choice. Movie stars, television, the latest box office smash—anything with glamour and glitz—that's what would attract teens according to the *Teen Spaces* advisory council. Following are some of their ideas for creating a space with star style:

Make the entry to the teen area look like the entrance to a movie theater, putting the name of the area and other important information in bright lights above the doorway.

Put stars on the floor with the names of the teens who assisted with the project. In the future, use this "walk of stars" as an award when teens do something special.

Go for the Brown Derby look, and hang framed caricatures or pictures of teens, library staff, and movie stars. The photos can be changed as stars and people come and go.

Frame movie posters outside the entrance to the area just as at the theater. Pick up posters for little or no cost at your local video store or movie theater. For added flair, incorporate in-house posters advertising library programs and events, new library materials, and so forth.

Include furnishings such as director chairs and comfy dressingroom-like couches and lounging chairs. Make study carrels look like dressing room tables by incorporating big mirrors with lights.

Incorporate a replica spotlight as an eye-catching accessory.

Add video store shelving and accessories. (See appendix B for a listing of suggested vendors.)

Use a red carpet to lead up to the reference or help desk.

Make Oscar-like stickers that can be affixed to or stuck out of books and materials you want to highlight. You might want to start with the "Teen's Choice" awards.

Use modern fixtures, curvilinear shapes, and flashes of exotic color that electrify.

The Campbell County Public Library in Gillette, Wyoming, consists of a young adult book area and a teen room. Relocation of the audiovisual department made room for this teen space created with the help of a teen advisory board. A donated couch, furnishings borrowed from other parts of the library, inexpensive lamps, a computer reserved for playing games, painted windows, a TV, VCR, CD player, and a teen-produced mural about Hollywood based on the Robert Frost poem "Provide Provide" define this library's teen area. Teens have the privilege of eating and drinking in their teen area. They can even have pizza delivered as long as they wait for it at the front door.

Music Theme

A music theme could celebrate music from the present and the past. Incorporate favorite musicians and groups. You could hang old sheet music, album covers, or CDs from the ceiling or mount them on the walls to form designs.

Nature Theme

For a nature theme, create an outdoor look indoors. Although a jungle safari might be a bit too juvenile, your teen council could come up with some creative twists.

Mural painted by teens in the Campbell County Library (Gillette, Wyoming)

Sports Theme

Because of the broad appeal and popularity of sports, it's a natural choice when trying to appeal to a broad group of teens. A sports theme could be inspired by local teams or athletes, by a variety of sports, or by major sporting events. For example, the twenty-member teen advisory board of Schaumburg (Illinois) Township District Library's teen center selected and developed a creative sports theme for their young adult space. The teen center in the Schaumburg Library was inspired by Wrigley Field (home of the Chicago Cubs baseball team) and the United Center in Chicago (where Michael Jordan played for the Chicago Bulls basketball team). The twenty-member teen advisory board selected the theme and chose features such as Astro Turf carpeting, a listening station, high school jerseys, ticket windows, electronic bulletin board, and more. Because the teen

center cannot be seen from the entrance of the youth services department, an additional neon sign is mounted in the opposite direction to guide teens to the area. An imitation turnstile stands below the entryway sign. On one wall the tops of the shelves are decorated to look like minilockers. The first names of the teen board members are slotted in the lockers, and the three area high school logos and the logo of the local minor league baseball team are positioned above. Three game tables were purchased and include game boards beneath the lacquer surface. (You can create game tables with the existing table in your library by simply buying the games of your choice and having a piece of Plexiglas or glass cut to fit over the top of the table to protect the game boards.)

Schaumburg (Illinois) Township District Library's entrance with ticket window display cases and large sign modeled after Wrigley Field

Schaumburg Library's brick wall, chain link fencing, and ivy

Developing a Design Style

If a thematic twist is not for your library, create an environment based on a particular design style. Go with a multidimensional feel by emphasizing three-dimensionality. Incorporate a variety of 3-D objects into a one-dimensional mural; hang items from the ceiling or, even better, mount them directly on the ceiling. Use everyday, fun objects as pieces of sculpture—big and small. Focus on images and elements based on their shape, not their context. Include them in the space because of the similarity in the way they look, not for their continuity in meaning (or vice versa for an entirely different look).

Another idea would be to use repetition throughout the space. Display a shape, an idea, or a popular motif (a repeated figure in a design) over and over again in different combinations, sizes, and colors. Color in itself could be a theme. Incorporate various shades and hues through different mediums. This is a highly effective method for adding personality and life to any space simply by being imaginative with paint and accessories.

Decorating 101

Teenagers and their interersts and tastes can be impulsive and unpredictable. Therefore, it is imperative that libraries decorate for teens in a versatile, interesting, and persuasive way. To be fully effective in achieving the goal of creating the "ideal" young adult space and meeting teen needs, we must educate ourselves about decorating concepts and practices. After that, it is our obligation to pass along this information to teens so they too can make well-informed decorating decisions for their library space. Issues to consider include creating a focal point; tackling walls, ceilings, and floors; color; the various decorative techniques, such as painting and wallpapering; texture considerations; lighting, furnishings, accessories, and layout.

To get teens involved, coordinate a series of field trips to visit other libraries with teen spaces, a mall, local bookstore, home remodeling center, a paint/wallpaper shop, or furniture store. On each trip, have teens carry a small clipboard that includes a simple questionnaire appropriate for each space visited. If possible, hand out disposable cameras so they can take pictures. If funds are short, have small groups share a camera. Have teens answer each questionnaire completely. The kinds of questions asked on each questionnaire will vary depending on the purpose of your visit. When visiting other teen spaces or stores in a mall or local bookstore, ask questions such as items 1 through 5 shown in figure 4.1. When visiting stores to pick out specific materials, have teens make note of specific items they liked (such as items 6 through 8 in figure 4.1). Give them guidelines, and be clear about what you want.

Collect questionnaires at the end of each trip. Have a trustworthy teen volunteer compile the results to be presented and discussed at the next focus group or advisory meeting. (Count all design meetings and field trips as young adult programs.)

TIP

To get teens involved, coordinate a series of field trips to visit other libraries with teen spaces, a mall, local bookstore, home remodeling center, a paint/wallpaper shop, or furniture store. On each trip, have teens carry a small clipboard that includes a simple questionnaire appropriate for each space visited.

FIGURE 4.1
Decorating Questionnaire for Teens

Name _____ Date _____ Store or place visited _____

Please record your responses or answers to all items that apply for this visit.

1. How did the space make you feel? _____
   _____

2. Did you like the
   walls?   ☐ yes ☐ no   Why or why not? _____
   _____

   floors?   ☐ yes ☐ no   Why or why not? _____
   _____

   ceiling?   ☐ yes ☐ no   Why or why not? _____
   _____

   lighting?   ☐ yes ☐ no   Why or why not?_____
   _____

   layout?   ☐ yes ☐ no   Why or why not? _____
   _____

   colors?   ☐ yes ☐ no   Why or why not? _____
   _____

3. Was the atmosphere warm and inviting? ☐ yes ☐ no   What made it that way?_____
   _____

4. What did you *like* most about this space (or place)? _____
   _____

5. What did you most *dislike* about the space (or place)? _____
   _____

6. What three paint colors did you like best? (Record their names and numbers. If possible, attach samples.)
   _____

7. What four pieces of furniture (couches, chairs, tables, etc.) did you like best? (Complete the following information for each.)

   Name   *Style*   *Order number*

   _____   _____   _____
   _____   _____   _____
   _____   _____   _____
   _____   _____   _____

8. What were your favorite items? (Draw a quick sketch of each or attach a photo.)

Design File

In addition to studying each of these decorating aspects, begin creating a design file to store all the information and ideas you have gathered. In fact, you may find that parts of the file, if you had started it at the onset of the project during the planning stages, could be used as a visual enhancement in your proposal. The purpose of a design file is to help you organize the project. It is an excellent way to illustrate ideas and is invaluable for making purchases and staying on top of the entire decorating phase of the project.

The physical file or the container can be almost anything—a three-ring binder (items may be hole punched when appropriate, topics can be separated with tabbed dividers, and file pocket may be inserted), an accordion-style folder with pockets, or a medium-sized file box with dividers. Use something that suits your personal working style, can be easily transported and simply organized, and is large enough to hold all samples and ideas. Also consider using something that will hold essential design tools such as a tape measure, notes, pens and pencils, tape, envelopes for quick storage of three-dimensional items, and a writing tablet.

In your design file, include the following items:

a floor plan

pictures of the space, including "before" shots and photographs throughout the course of the project from all angles

inspirational items: colors, textures, photos, images, and ideas (Include pictures from magazines, photocopies or scanned images from books, Internet printouts, and photographs of other inspirational teen spaces including library spaces, stores at the mall, and favorite teen hangouts.)

samples of paint, wallpaper, fabric, flooring (Staple or tape a small section of the item to a piece of cardboard or cardstock for easy, organized access.)

a calendar to keep track of important dates and deadlines

Once the final choices have been made, assemble your samples, photos, and materials on a piece of mat board or foam core. (Professionals often refer to this as a presentation board or a color board.) Ask a teen volunteer to assist in constructing the board. An 8 1/2-by-11-inch piece of white or black poster board or foam core will work best when creating a miniboard to be kept in the decorating file. If you are using the presentation board to make large group presentations, a poster-sized black or white board is most effective. This is great for presenting decorating plans to staff and administration and to teens at focus planning meetings. A professional designer should include this service in the contract.

Focal Point

Once you have determined a theme or design style, start thinking about establishing a focal point—something that will serve as the heart of the area, ultimately tying the space together. To begin, think of all the plans for the area and existing features of the space. Include items currently there as well as those elements that will eventually be added. What are or will be the most impressive components of the space? Keep in mind that the goal is to select something that will be the "heart" of the space. It should be the first thing that people notice when entering. It should also be something interesting to look at (whether visually or texturally appealing) and something that will accentuate the area's best qualities. Many times a focal point will be the largest element, but it could also be anything from a window to a piece of furniture to an entire wall. It could even be a view (if the teen area has a window with an breathtaking view). As you proceed with this process, consider the other elements of the area (walls, ceilings, floors, color, lighting, furniture, fixtures, accessories, and layout). They will work together to "frame" the focal point.

Walls, Ceilings, and Floors

No rule says that walls and ceilings have to be white. You might consider painting the ceiling the same color as the walls or, for a completely different effect, go a shade lighter. Since many libraries have suspended ceilings, attempting to be creative with ceilings might be somewhat of a challenge. For those who are lucky enough to have a drywall ceiling, try something different with paint and 3-D objects. You can even create something out of this world by painting a mural on the ceiling. Wallpaper borders are another easy and inventive way to jazz up walls and ceilings. Mount ready-made borders along the edge of the ceiling or along the middle of walls. Or, better yet, create your own borders by cutting out designs from scrap wallpaper, magazines, or whatever comes to mind and then decoupage them directly to walls and ceilings. If your library has high ceilings and you want them to appear lower, create the illusion of a lower ceiling by placing a border directly on the wall several inches below the ceiling, or paint the ceiling a darker shade of the wall color. By the same token, you can create the illusion of a higher ceiling by placing a border at the very top of the wall where it meets the ceiling or by painting the ceiling a light shade (but not necessarily white).

The flooring found in most libraries is fairly typical of business flooring. It's made to be durable and to hide the dirt as much as possible. Most commonly, floors are either carpeted or wooden. If you are constructing a new young adult space, define the area with a different color or patterned carpet from that of the other library areas. Inlaid carpet is another attractive flooring option. Pretty much anything can be done with carpet as long as your library's budget can afford it. Carpet tiles are another good option if there are concerns about future stains and wear because tiles can easily be replaced. Also, if designed properly, tiles used to create a pattern in the floor will do wonders for hiding dirt and wear. Overall, carpeting is a great choice for a teen area because it lends itself to imagination, and it is definitely the most comfortable of floor treatments. (Teens need the option to be able to spread out on the ground.)

If carpeted floors are not an option for your library, other flooring, whether wood, tile, or vinyl/linoleum, can be easily dressed up with area rugs or a little paint. You can do amazing things both decoratively and texturally with faux finishes and stencils. Furthermore, area rugs are a "must have" for any teen space. Besides making great accent pieces, area rugs are affordable, add color and variety, and can be used in conjunction with any other type of floor treatment.

Color

Whether addressing the topic of walls, ceilings, floors, or furnishings, one of the easiest and most dramatic ways to create an impact in a space is to use color effectively. Color reflects personality, mood, and interest, setting the scene for any area. It is important not to be afraid of color, especially when it comes to decorating for teenagers; instead, think unconventional and "fresh," never hesitating to be unique. Choose colors that excite and motivate you and your teen partners. Don't put off color decisions to the end of the project; start collecting ideas and swatches at the beginning. Look for images and items that "decoratively" motivate you and your teen collaborators. Ideas could originate from a picture in a magazine, a fabric or paint swatch, a crayon, or maybe even from a preexisting element in the library or whatever is serving as the area's focal point. Keep the "inspirational" item (or a photo of the item if it is too large to conveniently transport) readily available to take shopping or to meetings with vendors or designers so it can be compared with color samples, fabric, wallpaper, and furnishings. Having it with you at all times will save hours of frustration and time and provide guidance when choosing the remaining elements of the space.

Colors can convey a wide range of feelings, ideas, and meanings. When choosing a color scheme, plan creatively. To do this, it's important to acquire a basic awareness of the nuances of color and the effects that can be created with it. Here's a quick guide:

Red, yellow, blue are known as primary colors. They cannot be produced from a combination of other pigments.

Secondary colors are a result of mixing two primary colors. That is, red and yellow make orange; yellow and blue make green; blue and red make purple or violet.

Colors beyond primary and secondary colors are known as tertiary colors.

Complementary colors are those colors that are opposite each other on the color wheel. For example, red is a complement to green, and yellow is a complement to purple and vice versa. (Color wheels can be readily located in many paint and decorating books and web pages. See appendix B for suggestions.)

Neutrals include white, black, variations of gray, and beige tones.

Yellow, red, and orange are considered warm, lively colors.

Blue, green, and violet/purple are regarded as cool, calm colors.

Soft colors generally relay quiet contemplation, sophistication, and relaxation.

Bright colors normally stimulate and communicate a modern and playful mood.

Color can have an impact on the proportions of a space, making it feel bigger or smaller than what it truly is. To give the illusion of a larger space, use a monochromatic, light, cool-color scheme or patterns with small print. Blue is a good choice when attempting to increase the feeling of space. Use dark, bold, warm colors or prints to create a cozy feel. Produce a similar comfy feeling by choosing the same color (something other than white) for both the walls and the ceiling. The greater the contrast in color, the smaller and cozier the room will look. To make a ceiling look higher, use white paint or a light color.

When using a fabric swatch to help determine wall color, the background color of the fabric is generally a good choice. A lesser, even more predominant, color in the swatch would be a better choice for accents or furnishings.

The more intense a color, the more it is noticed. You can add a glaze or glossy finish to a surface to make a color look even brighter.

The more you learn about the benefits of color and how it can breathe life into a space, the more difficult it will be to accept the traditional library idea of white walls, white ceiling, white everything. Color represents energy, and energy is a necessary component of the ideal teen space. A young adult area is not the place to introduce conservative décor, but if a conventional scheme is a requirement at your library, lighter shades are a better alternative to plain white. If you simply cannot get away from "white walls and white ceiling," experiment with a palette of bright colors for trim work, accents, and accessories (posters, throw rugs, pillows, etc.).

When choosing colors, don't be afraid to experiment with multiple shades and patterns, but be cautious about choosing too many colors for a single space or it could result in an unbalanced effect. (A maximum of three colors for each space is good practice.) It can also be fun to explore different avenues by mixing your own paint colors, keeping in mind that it's easiest to mix colors in the same color family. Before making any final selections, always view wall colors and treatments vertically against the wall and floor colors and treatments flat on the floor. Look at the samples at various times of the day and evening to make sure the patterns and colors work well in the space at all times. Also be aware that color is part of everything that makes the space—including furniture, fabrics, and accessories.

Paint and Other Treatments

Once a color scheme has been determined, decide what materials and techniques will be used to express the ideas and colors of choice. The most common approach is to paint the area because paint is inexpensive and easy to apply and can completely transform a room in minutes. Paint finishes and techniques such as stenciling, sponging, colorwashing, ragging, combing, and mural painting are also great ways to add interest and color, and best of all, they can be applied to almost any surface. Although wallpaper and wallpaper borders are usually more expensive and more difficult to apply than paint, they nonetheless are both fabulous treatments that have the potential for creating a tremendous impact. A similar concept to wallpapering, decoupage is a wonderful method for adding bursts of color and interesting detail to a space. Unlike wallpaper, it is relatively inexpensive and can be applied to practically any surface. Regardless of the treatment, always think in terms of the desired style and atmosphere of the space, and never be confined to one technique, pattern, or color.

Painting

Paint can be applied to most anything as long it is the appropriate type of paint for the surface and the surface is prepared properly. Paint is so readily available in thousands of colors and varieties that it is the most versatile element of the décor. Therefore, it is wise to make a final paint decision in conjunction with the other elements of the teen area (flooring, fabrics, and furnishings). When selecting a paint color, have your design file handy so you can easily refer to swatches from the other elements of the room. If you don't have a professional with whom to consult, ask a salesperson at the hardware, paint, or home improvement store for advice. In addition to giving helpful paint tips, many of these stores also offer custom color mixing, which enables a customer to bring in just about any color reference and have paint mixed to match. Web sites are another easy resource for general paint information and advice. For more details, see appendix B.

As with any wall, fabric, or floor treatment, before making a final decision about a paint color, it is wise to do the following:

1. Tape a selection of your favorite paint chips directly on the wall in the teen area. A strip of paint chips is generally best because there are multiple shades of a color on one card. This is helpful in viewing underlying tones and providing a good overall assessment of the color.

2. Once the selection is narrowed down, purchase sample bottles or pints of your colors, and paint test patches on the wall in the teen area (generally a 12- or 48-inch square will do). For a less permanent test, paint the same size square on a board, and hang the board on the wall. This test will provide a true idea of what the colors will look like in their environment. When testing paint (or any decorating element for that matter), it is important to "live with it" for a few days to make certain it looks the way you want it to look. Remember that the larger the painted area, the more intense the color will seem.

3. Make sure the paint dries thoroughly before approving or rejecting it. Paint always looks different when it's wet than when it's dry.

4. Always double check paint colors against the other elements of the space, including fabric samples and floor coverings.

5. When the sampling is over, if the color is not right for the space, simply choose another color and try again.

Special Techniques

Paint color alone can be a pretty powerful decorating tool, oftentimes perfectly conveying the theme of a space and providing a brilliant end result, but for those times when the area demands something beyond color or a bit more unusual, consider trying a special painting technique. Blackboard paint can turn a wall or part of a wall into a nonpermanent canvas for teen creativity. Fluorescent paint or metallic finishes might be a bit too much for an entire room but work well as accents. Sponging, rag rolling, crackling, and stenciling are all great for adding texture and interest to any space. They are also excellent for concealing a world of imperfections on walls and furnishings alike. (Refer to appendix B for helpful decorating resources.)

Once a paint color and technique are chosen, estimate how much paint you will need to complete the job. Multiply the length of each wall by its height and add the products of all walls to find the total number of square feet. Divide the total square feet by the number of square feet a gallon of paint will cover to determine the number of gallons needed for one coat. Plan on doubling this figure because it's more than likely that two coats of paint will be necessary. (Three coats may be required depending on the color choice and condition of the walls.) Take into consideration that this method of figuring gallons needed may differ slightly if you are applying a faux finish or using a special painting technique.

Mural Art

A mural may consist of a small image in a corner or even a full wall panorama. Although usually applied to walls, murals can also work on furniture, doors, ceilings, and floors. Work with teen volunteers or art students to create and paint your mural. Check with your local middle and high school art departments.

An overhead projector is an excellent tool for mural projects. It enlarges the images so they can be traced and painted. Have students create their drawings in art class and then transfer the images to transparencies and project them on the walls. This will allow you to be creative with placement and size before anything is permanently painted. Once it's been determined where the images will reside, students can trace the art in pencil and then paint it. Freehand work is always an option as long as the idea is well planned out and the images are penciled on the wall before painting.

If permanence of a mural is an issue, create paintings on a large, stretched canvas or boards and hang them on the walls or from the ceiling or at the end of shelving ranges. Again, this has potential for a class project or an after-school art club undertaking. Have teens work with the teacher to develop a theme or a general idea for the mural. Each student can be responsible for developing a different piece of the mural. Each year Cheryl Kuonen, teen librarian at the Mentor Public Library (Mentor, Ohio), has local art students create two-toned oversized paintings of famous actors and singers (3 feet by 3 feet) in the classroom. Each year approximately four paintings are done to cover the walls in the library. This is a great way to add excitement and keep up-to-date. To see a few sample murals, look at the photos for Phelps Community Memorial Library, Marion Public Library, Campbell County Public Library, and Schaumburg Township District Library in the themes section earlier in this chapter.

Trompe l'Oeil

You can generate a 3-D feel with paint using trompe l'oeil (a French term that means, "to fool the eye"). This type of painting is rendered so realistically that the viewer is temporarily tricked into perceiving that the viewed objects are real. In a convincing trompe l'oeil, some of the objects even seem to project themselves into the space.

For example, if there aren't any windows in your young adult room, you could paint a corner of the space to look like there is a gaping hole through which you can see what's outside the building either in the near or far distance.

Wallpaper

Wallpaper is traditionally more expensive and time consuming to apply than paint, but it is also a terrific decorating tool that can dramatically change a room's appearance overnight. Like textured paint and various painting techniques, wallpaper is great for covering up a multitude of imperfections or an existing wall treatment that is less than desirable. If the walls of the teen area are covered with paneling and it's out of the question to remove it and redo the walls, then wallpaper could be the option for you (although paint works well in this situation too). If you like the look of wallpaper but are on a limited budget, consider wallpapering one wall as an accent wall or use wallpaper borders as a less expensive alternative to wallpapering an entire room. Consider asking teens to make their own wallpaper by cutting out shapes or images and decoupaging them to the wall either in a fixed pattern or in a collage style.

As with paint, traditional wallpaper choices can be overwhelming. When selecting and ordering wallpaper, keep the following in mind:

TIP

Consider asking teens to make their own wallpaper by cutting out shapes or images and decoupaging them to the wall either in a fixed pattern or in a collage style.

Color and pattern will always be *the most* important deciding factors.

Consider wallpapers that are durable, washable, prepasted, and pretrimmed.

Select a variety of wallpaper samples and take them back to the teen area to tape on the wall. This will give you an idea of what the colors and patterns will look like in their new environment.

Avoid choosing thin, cheap paper because it will tear easily and be a nightmare to hang.

Large-print wallpaper will make a room seem cozier.

Vertical patterns make ceilings seem higher.

In old buildings, the walls, windows, and doors are often not "plumb" or perfectly vertical. This makes wallpapering more difficult, so try to stay away from vertical patterns in these instances.

Before ordering wallpaper make sure to carefully and accurately measure the area, taking into account doorways, windows, and any other space where wallpaper will not be present.

Paper is always sold in double-roll bolts, but measuring and ordering is done by single-roll increments generally 15 feet long. Roll width varies from 20-1/2 inches to 35 inches.

When ordering and receiving wallpaper, make sure that all the rolls have the same lot number. Before hanging the paper, always compare the shade/color of rolls to make sure they match.

Always paint the trim in the room before hanging wallpaper.

For best adhesion, use diluted paste when hanging prepasted paper.

Begin hanging wallpaper in the most inconspicuous corner and work around the space in one direction.

For helpful resources on selecting wallpaper, calculating coverage, and hanging tips, refer to appendix B.

Texture

Texture is an element that is often overlooked by the amateur decorator. This is unfortunate because texture is an essential component of every décor. It pulls a space together, stimulating the eye, adding depth to an ordinarily flat space, and creating an exciting and interesting overall effect—exactly what the ideal teen area needs. Texture also provides variety and contrast and accents the colors and overall feel of the space. It can be introduced to an area through wall treatments, fabric, carpeting, and elements such as wood, tile, glass, and metal. Such elements not only add texture but they also convey atmosphere. For instance, due to its tone and grain, wood suggests a warm and cozy feeling. In contrast, hard, glossy finishes can impart a more modern and, sometimes, cold feeling.

When incorporating texture into a teen area ask, "What is the theme of the space, and what textural elements could be incorporated to better convey it?" To be successful with texture, it is essential to stop thinking in two dimensions and to remember that texture is not a difficult concept. In fact, it's easy because textural variety can be achieved in so many ways. If you consider the color of the item at hand and select things with interesting surfaces and fabrics, you'll never go wrong. Start by looking at the walls (or ceilings, for that matter). Texture can be easily incorporated using a faux painting technique, by hanging art or three-dimensional items, or by suspending objects from the ceiling. Another great idea for a wall or ceiling treatment that adds lots of texture is to mount CDs on the wall or hang them from the ceiling (use old discs, the freebies you get in the mail, or purchase blank ones in packs of 50 or 100). Just use a little spray or liquid adhesive to attach them.

Laura Gruniger, young adult librarian at the Lawrence Headquarters of Mercer County Library System in Lawrenceville, New Jersey, provides a wonderful example of what it's like to create a room with interest, style, and texture on a limited budget. Typical of young adult space projects, Gruniger's plan did not start out as an endeavor to make over her library's teen area but that is how it soon ended up. In addition to sprucing up the existing 15-foot-by-45-foot young adult area, a former small typing room adjacent to the young adult space was renovated and transformed into a 9-foot-by-11-foot young adult activity room. The activity room is a fairly small space but perfect for a teen hangout, group studying, and small programs. The best part, Gruniger adds, is, "Teens respect it as their own!"

The highlight of this teen space is its inspired use of texture and accessories. The little things make the space what it is—great! The activity room walls were painted a vibrant, denim blue (a nice touch since the larger adjoining young adult space located in the library proper is painted cream). Within the activity room, there's a worktable with seating for four, four padded chairs, a sleek footstool, and shelving for miscellaneous materials and games. In contrast to the activity room, Gruniger was faced with a fairly conservative décor in the existing larger young adult space, so she decided to get creative with accessories and nonpermanent fixtures to add color and energy to the static environment.

Trendy wall art, teen-developed collages, brightly colored throw rugs and pillows, homemade window treatments, artificial trees, posters, doorway beads, wind chimes, unusual light fixtures, and interactive knick-knacks such as snow

Mercer County Library System (Lawrenceville, New Jersey)
Young adult activity room with accessories and the main
young adult area

globes, a sculpture, a magnetic spinner for program advertising, a mini Zen garden, an oversized fish pillow, an aquarium, a small fountain, and a funhouse
mirror all blend perfectly in the Mercer County Library System's teen area to
make a creative, exciting haven for teens. A semicircular seat made from a left-
over circulation desk piece is covered with masses of inexpensive, brightly colored pillows. (A large pillowtop cushion might be another option that would
also create a practical yet comfortable lounging/reading area for teens.) Overall,
Gruniger says her library's young adult space is, "Fun, trendy, and unlibrary-
like—teens love it." For more information on Gruniger's library see the section
"Something Old, Something New" later in this chapter as well as appendix C
for a complete listing of all the *Teen Spaces* resource libraries.

Lighting

Like texture, lighting is one of those decorating elements that many times gets
overlooked. Most people do not immediately recognize the importance and
effects of a good lighting plan. Lighting is crucial in a teen area primarily
because teens will be spending a large amount of time studying there. Lighting
also creates atmosphere, which directly affects the mood, appearance, and function of a space. For instance, lighting can play a key role in making a small room

appear larger. If this is the case in your library, plan on incorporating a combination of as much natural and artificial light as possible. Mirrors are also quite effective in creating the illusion of a large space.

"Excellent lighting has everything to do with the visual appeal of the space," says Peter Gisolfi, the architect who designed the media center at Horace Greeley High School in Chappaqua, New York, in 1996. He recommends mixed lighting for pleasant, glare-free illumination. At Horace Greeley, he incorporated a broad window exposure with large, operable windows that provide natural light by day in the reading and reference areas. He also used a wide variety of electric light sources including the following:

pendant fluorescent fixtures at the stacks and in the media
    center classroom

pendant incandescent fixtures at the circulation desk

fluorescent sconces on the brick piers throughout

pendant compact fluorescents in the main reading/reference area

incandescent table lamps on the reading tables

adjustable halogen spots to light the art on the walls[7]

From this example alone, it is evident that the topic of lighting can be a complicated one with the potential for a great deal of planning. The variety of lighting fixtures and styles are enough to overwhelm anyone. Any designer will tell you that each type has its pluses and minuses, but it all comes down to the mood you want to create in combination with the practical application and function of the space.

Because of the overwhelming number of fixtures and the intricacies of creating a good lighting plan, it is a good idea to acquire the services of a professional if you are planning any major lighting renovations. It will be that person's job to suggest the most appropriate and effective lighting options for a teen area based on its functions and its clientele. If you have already hired a professional design company, a lighting plan will be included in its services. If you have decided not to hire a professional, consider paying for a consultation with a contractor or a lighting designer—it will be worth the money. If your budget precludes you from hiring a lighting expert, get the input of a specialist at a lighting or home improvement store. A good solution for a small-scale lighting project is to incorporate freestanding lighting fixtures such as lamps for ambient (mood) lighting and do-it-yourself up-lights for task (work-oriented) lighting.

Although practical lights are essential, don't forget about novelty lighting. Such items would include disco balls, mirror balls, belt lighting (theater marquee look), rotating beacon lights (similar to those on a police car), neon lights, and rope lighting. In an unusual use of lighting, the Burton Barr Central Library of the Phoenix (Arizona) Public Library incorporated fiber optic lighting that changes color throughout the ceiling in its "Teen Central." (See photos later in this chapter.)

Furniture

When it comes to furniture, comfort and style rank high in making a teen area unique and inviting. This is an exciting time for teens in the library as well as in the furniture marketplace. Similar to libraries, more and more furniture companies are looking to teenagers and what they need and want. As a result, many new lines have been developed specifically for this age group. Not only does this mean more choices for libraries purchasing new furnishings, it also means more inspirational ideas for those redoing old furniture.

Teens have a lot to say about furniture. In fact, it's high on their list of priorities and is distinctly reflected in their ideas and feelings about library spaces. Teens everywhere are asking for that one simple thing—comfort. They want comfortable furniture for hanging out in as well as for studying; therefore, it's crucial that comfortable furnishings play a large part in the space plan. When the *Teen Spaces* advisory board was asked to define comfort, members responded with the following descriptions:

squishiness

you can curl up in a ball and be comfy in it

color

plushness and softness

you're able to fall into it

cushions and lots of pillows

it contours for back support

you don't have to share it

having fluff inside

it doesn't hurt your butt

roominess

something or someplace that makes you feel
    like you are at home and welcome

Even those libraries that have "good" teen areas often lack in this one special (and perfectly reasonable) comfort element. After she transformed a corner of a 1915 library building into a fabulous and progressive teen space, Vicky Pratt, young adult librarian at the Swampscott Public Library in Massachusetts, says that teens still request, "a larger space with more 'comfy' couches.'"[8] In Wanda Higgins's article, "What Do Young Adults Want in Their School Library," she mentions first and foremost, "the library should be a place with comfortable furniture and a welcoming atmosphere, where students can feel safe, secure, and relaxed."[9] She suggests that the school library should have areas designated for different functions, and it's important that one of those areas be a place with overstuffed chairs, pillows, and low tables—a place where they can lay on the floor and stretch out like they do at home.

Just take a look at what the Carmel (Indiana) High School has done. A large library media center, this facility ascends four levels. It includes well-defined work and gathering areas and a large casual reading area that is open, airy, roomy, and full of windows. In addition to sled-based chairs for traditional study tables, this library incorporates casual lounge furniture and ottomans. It is clear that comfort is key in both public and school environments. Teens everywhere are requesting it and librarians everywhere should be including it.

Carmel (Indiana) High School Library casual reading area

Results from surveys and discussions with the *Teen Spaces* advisory council that asked, "What kind of furniture do you like to sit in?" were compiled and compared with results from polls and focus group discussions conducted at the Phoenix (Arizona) Public Library. The groups said they wanted

soft, inviting, comfy stuff

anything cushiony

couches and loveseats (especially big,
    squishy ones with lots of pillows)

beanbag chairs

anything with pillows

massaging chairs

comfortable chairs and couches
    (like the ones at Barnes and Noble)

deep arm chairs

leather furniture

recliners

chairs that spin

velour/velvet chairs

inflatable chairs

overstuffed chairs[10]

The *Teen Spaces* advisory council also stressed that being able to sit comfortably on the floor is important as well as having study tables that are large enough to spread out at with chairs comfortable enough to study in for long periods of time.

When asked why they like these furnishings, both groups responded:

When something is soft, you can just hang all over it.

It's relaxing!

It's important that something feels good when you sit on it.

You can curl up into a ball and be comfy.

It's easy to get comfortable so you're not squirmy.

Couches are versatile—one person can stretch out or five people can squeeze in.

Good furniture molds to your body.

With so much stress, you need furniture that is relaxing.

The Phoenix (Arizona) Public Library is a new construction project that produced a wonderful teen space. The area includes

furnishings from Urbanese, Goodmans, Diva, and Linea

large projection screen for videos and DVDs

20 Internet computers with flat screen LCD monitors

café area with vending machines

surround-sound

concrete dance floor surrounded by beanbag chairs

fiber optic and other unusual lighting (by Lightspot)

private desk areas

portable art gallery

large tables for group work

glass-enclosed study rooms

Lounging area with ultracomfortable furnishings in the teen area of the Burton Barr Central Library, Phoenix (Arizona) Public Library

The café area in the teen area of the Burton Barr Central Library, Phoenix Public Library (Arizona)

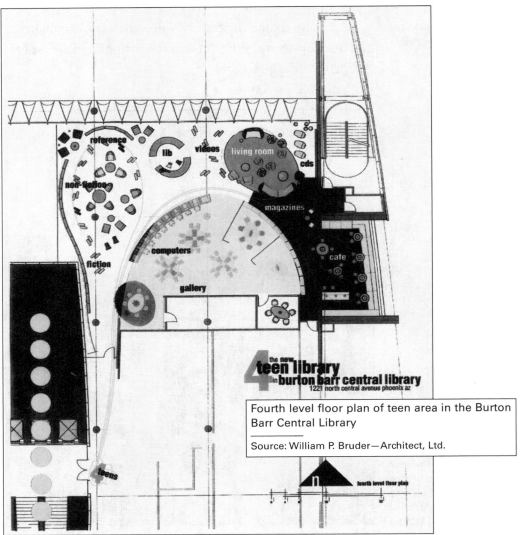

Fourth level floor plan of teen area in the Burton Barr Central Library

Source: William P. Bruder—Architect, Ltd.

The Los Angeles Public Library Teen'Scape
Living Room with a series of study rooms
© Los Angeles Public Library; photo:
Tom Bonner

The Los Angeles Public Library's Teen'Scape is another ultimate example of comfortable seating. In March 2000, Teen'Scape expanded into its current site. (The name "Teen'Scape" is meant to convey both sanctuary for and ownership by teenagers.)

Los Angeles Public Library's Teen'Scape Living Room
© Los Angeles Public Library; photo: Tom Bonner

The Los Angeles Public Library Teen'Scape Cyber Space area
© Los Angeles Public Library; photo: Tom Bonner

Something Old, Something New

Looking at your original furniture list created in chapter 2, what are your plans in regard to new furnishings? Are you considering reusing existing furniture from the former young adult area? Is there something from another area in the library that has caught your eye that you'd like to revamp and relocate to teen services? Even if your initial plans involved all new furnishings, you might change your mind after considering the possibilities for "recycled" furniture. If you are on a limited budget, it helps to be a scavenger. Look for things elsewhere in the library that could be transplanted to the teen area. Keep your eye out for things in unexpected places. Laura Gruniger at the Mercer County Public Library (Lawrenceville, New Jersey) found many of the items in her teen area for free or very little money. (See the photos earlier in this chapter.)

Gruniger rearranged the existing library chairs and tables and stapled some coordinating fabric onto the old chairs. The chairs coordinate with the fabric on the window and bulletin board (found in the library's attic). These items can be updated at minimal cost. A revolving wire rack that had been donated by a local company was spray-painted in metallic blue. A blue countertop, left over from another branch's renovation project, was installed in the teen activity room. An old circulation desk (again from a branch renovation) was turned into a bench. In addition, Gruniger incorporated the following things:

- A dressmaker's dummy abandoned by a long-retired branch manager was used for display as well as for the haunted library program.
- An aquarium was found at a yard sale for $40. It included the thirty-gallon tank, filter, plants, bubble rod, gravel, rocks, skull, and other items. The stand for the aquarium was in the library's storage. (The Friends of the Library buy the water conditioner and filter accessories.) Although it's a lot of maintenance, the aquariam is a pleasing addition to the library. (This could be a great project for a teen group from both a financial and maintenance perspective.)
- An unsealed table fountain was purchased for $7. It's soothing and eye-catching.
- On one of her regular visits to the teen stores at the malls for clearance items Gruniger found an entire roll of blacklight paper for $2 because it was a bit torn.
- A giant fish pillow was found for $12 (Gruniger claims to have "splurged" on this item but it was a big hit and well worth the investment.)
- A mini funhouse mirror was purchased for $4 and is used to post information. (Note: the mirrors can be purchased in bulk to decorate a whole wall.)

Because a few items have been stolen, Gruniger says she never spends more than a few dollars on anything. In addition to the sources Gruniger used, you might check an organization such as Gifts in Kind International to find out about obtaining free furnishings, accessories, and supplies for nonprofit organizations. (See appendix B.)

Giving life to old furniture can be a very creative and rewarding undertaking for you and teen collaborators. Many would assume that furniture face-lifts are reserved for those on a small budget. Although reusing fixed-up furniture is a wise investment for libraries with limited funds, it can be an equally beneficial experience for larger, well-funded organizations. It's all about tapping the imagination of teens and drawing on their talents to breathe life into old, tired furniture and fixtures.

A new coat of paint can do wonders for an old piece of furniture. Mini-murals and decoupage are also exceptional ways to add colorful touches and interest to chairs, tables, and shelving. For example, you could take a wooden bench and turn it into a piece of art by painting a minimural on the seat and down the side of the leg. In 1999, two staff members and a young adult advisory board at the Lawrence (Kansas) Public Library set out to redesign their teen space by carving out a niche distinctly denoted by inlaid carpet, a large electric sign proclaiming "The Zone," and comfortable chairs throughout. Those teens also transformed a plain reading bench into a piece of art.

Tabletops are the perfect canvas for a mural or a collage. They can also be converted into game tables by purchasing or painting game boards on tabletops and protecting them with a custom-cut piece of glass or Plexiglas as they did at the Schaumburg (Illinois) Township District Library.

If you're stuck with old lounging chairs that are dirty and worn out or are covered with outdated fabric, see if they can easily be reupholstered in-house by you and your young adult team. If not, try budgeting for a professional to redo them. A little fabric in the right colors and prints can give a space a whole new look. If money is tight, consider having one or two items done at a time.

Another option for fixing up old furniture is to collect pieces from flea markets, thrift shops, and garage sales. You might want to leave some things just as you bought them. Others will have to be touched up, painted, or decoupaged—whatever you can dream up. Buying secondhand furniture is quickly gaining

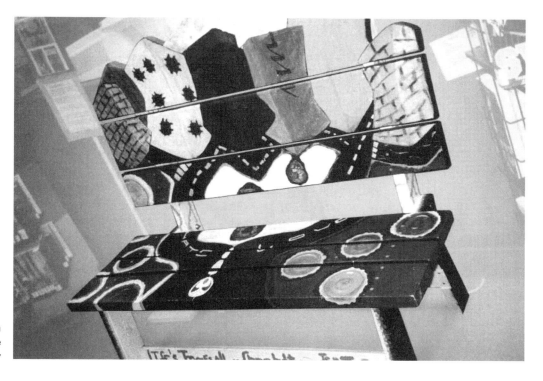

Teen-decorated bench
at the Lawrence
(Kansas) Public Library

popularity with librarians who want to do something with their teen area but are on a limited budget. Even well-funded libraries have discovered that flea market finds can lead to great interactive projects for teens as well as add a lot of interest to young adult spaces. What a great outing for a teen advisory council or focus group: spending a Saturday afternoon learning how to be resourceful and looking for the perfect bargain with the idea that they will be able to use their creativity to turn the items into treasures for the new teen area.

TIP

Even well-funded libraries have discovered that flea market finds can lead to great interactive projects for teens as well as add a lot of interest to young adult spaces. What a great outing for a teen advisory council or focus group: spending a Saturday afternoon learning how to be resourceful and looking for the perfect bargain with the idea that they will be able to use their creativity to turn the items into treasures for the new teen area.

Study Furniture

When selecting new furnishings for a teen area, think tough, portable, and attractive. Items need to be durable as well as functional and visually appealing. Opt for furniture that will look fresh and up-to-date for a significant period of time, and select items based on what teens are actually asking for, not on what you guess or perceive they want. Pieces chosen should help define and enhance the theme or style of the area, not distract from it. Be wise with purchases, and don't be afraid to invest in good quality furniture. Making good choices now will help build a strong, long-lasting foundation for the space.

To get started, think back to those things teens most want in their library, the general nature of teens, and their love for lounging. A combination of both lounge-style seating and study furnishings is a requirement for the ideal teen area. No matter how small the space, there are always ways to incorporate both. Adding comfortable furniture doesn't have to mean that you squeeze in a couch. If you are limited on space or funds, come up with alternative solutions like incorporating small, nontraditional library tables for studying and futons or butterfly chairs for lounging. If there is no possible way to fit in both types of seating, concentrate on comfort in the teen space proper and encouraging studying in an adjacent area. Better yet, look around your library for a niche or room that doesn't get much use and transform it into a "teen lounge." Keep in mind—it's all about being inventive and resourceful.

Tables and chairs traditionally designated as "study" furniture should be purchased with the intention that teens will want to use them for one of two things: to sit by themselves to study or to sit in small groups to work together. "Study" furnishings are a tricky topic because research indicates that teens prefer to study in comfortable furniture, but there are those instances when they need traditional tables and chairs. (Look again at the photos of the Swampscott and Mercer County Libraries earlier in this chapter.) Following are the most important things to keep in mind when selecting study furniture:

Select chairs that are comfortable to sit in and tables that are easy to work at. When choosing computer furnishings, make sure they are easily accessible and ergonomically designed.

Choose items that go along with the décor and feel of the rest of the space. Select study furniture that complements the lounge-type furniture. For example, traditional, hardwood library furniture generally does not work well in a space with a contemporary design.

Look to library vendors such as Gaylord, Brodart, Demco, or Highsmith for traditional furnishings but also consult with nonlibrary vendors when making purchases. Home furnishing and large chain stores are great furniture resources. (See appendix B.) Also, don't forget about garage sales and consignment shops for low-cost, creative ideas.

Fixtures

A number of miscellaneous items fall under the fixtures category: shelving units, paperback spinners, display racks, and freestanding display units. Once you know how many shelves you need in the space (refer to chapters 2 and 3), start thinking about how they will decoratively fit into the space. For example, traditional metal library shelves can be combined with lift-up shelves for magazines, end-of-the-range displays for merchandising, and bookstore-like units such as slant shelving and zigzag shelving. If new shelving is out of the question, try painting your existing shelves with a good quality metal paint; in fact, the end panels are great places for murals. If you have the budget, go for something completely different. For example, the Phoenix Public Library's shelves are 66 inches high and made of fiberglass and stainless steel. The fiberglass shelves are yellow, orange, and grape to coordinate with the rest of the room. Besides standard shelving considerations, many of the items in the fixture category fall under the heading of "merchandising tools." (Refer to chapter 5 and to appendix B for fixture suggestions and tips.)

Accessories

You will want to strategically integrate accessories to enhance a teen area. These added extras are an easy and inexpensive way to add kick to any space. To successfully accessorize, include elements that energize the overall look and feel of the space. Although these items are generally decorative, they could also include things that simply convey that this is a teen area.

Rely on what you see in teens' personal surroundings (their bedrooms, lockers, etc.) to help develop accessory ideas for the space. For example, the most popular decorative teen accessories are pillows. A young adult area is not complete without pillows. It's comfort teens are after and pillows are the ultimate comfort provider—the bigger and squishier the better. Besides offering comfort and bursts of color, pillows are inexpensive. How about making pillows out of old t-shirts? What a low-cost, stylish, and personalized solution.

Posters fall close behind pillows in accessories treasured by teens. Versatile and inexpensive, posters can be changed periodically to reflect new styles and interests. Hang them as is or in frames, directly on the walls or on the ceiling. Try something different and arrange them in unusual ways, at angles, overlapping in a collage, or side by side in a long row. Movie theaters are a great source of inspiration. For example, the Allen County Public Library simply and effectively used the American Library Association's Read posters. Another spin on the idea is that of North Central High School (Indianapolis, Indiana), which created similar posters entitled "Got Book?" These life-sized pictures feature faculty holding their favorite books. Accessories such as these are a great way to let teens know that the adults can have fun too.

Another example of accessorizing is the Robert Cormier Center for Young Adults at the Leominster (Massachusetts) Public Library. It has the look and feel of a typical teen's bedroom. In this renovation project, teens chose the colors and furnishings, designed the lounging area, and created a mural focusing on Robert Cormier's life in Leominster. This teen area is filled with visual stimulation including cartoons, posters, and jam-packed bulletin boards. A reading loft incorporated into the space creates a private area littered with pillows. Figurines, knickknacks, and animated toys highlight the librarian's desk and her sense of fun, and a ministereo with a CD player and wall-mounted speakers (music is always on when the Center is open), comfy furniture, and Sauder PlyLok study chairs complete the space.

Other interesting accessories include the following:

bulletin boards, which are great for poster displays, teen-related happenings (wrap them in fabric or paint them for something different)

an oversized white board or other medium where things can be written and teens can be creative and produce temporary graffiti

plastic crates as an alternative for shelving and displays (but they're not always sturdy)

framed art, whether teen originals or famous reproductions to which teens relate and that complement the colors, theme, and style of the space

sculpture or three-dimensional, everyday objects (sports equipment, teen toys, fish tanks, etc.)

snack machines

games, including chess, checkers, and a variety of popular board games (either built in, as at the Schaumburg Township District Library, or as part of the collection, available for in-house use as well as for loan)

wastebaskets and office supplies (pencils, pens, paper, staplers, tape)

library materials (For more information on visual merchandising, see chapter 5.)

Art is another great accessory. Commission young artists to create paintings or sculptures. To house the art, consider purchasing frames for the paintings, and set aside a wall or corner of the area to serve as a "gallery" space. Incorporate sculpture throughout the space, locating more fragile elements on top of bookcases out of reach, or purchase a wall-mounted or freestanding

TIP

Commission young artists to create murals, paintings, or sculptures.

ALA Read posters on the soffet near the reference desk and slat wall panels highlight materials at the end of each shelving range at the Allen County Public Library (Fort Wayne, Indiana)

A comfortable corner of the Leominster (Massachusetts) Public Library

The teen-designed loft area with floor pillows, posters, and black paint at Leominster Public Library

showcase. Another option would be to work with art teachers to produce art and volunteer the library to serve as a gallery for traveling art shows. The Peabody Institute in Massachusetts regularly houses middle and high school art displays, which helps decorate the space and gets teens to visit.

Layout

When laying out a teen area, consider the traffic pattern of the space as well as the activities that will take place there. The arrangement should enhance, not hinder, an area's accessibility and atmosphere. This is the point in the project where you pull everything together. Begin laying out the space by working around the focal point. Pay close attention to balance and how the focal point ties into the rest of the space. Place large pieces (furniture, shelving) in the space first. Be aware of the light in the room when placing pieces associated with studying or reading. Keep pieces of similar scale together, but remember that something a little off-balance and unusual is oftentimes better than that which is too conventional or symmetrical.

Use the layout of a space to assist in delineating separate areas for studying and socializing. Creative furniture placement or the addition of room dividers (such as folding screens or office panels) can instantly separate an area into two distinctive spaces. Depending on the features and design of the area, a few hooks in the ceiling, a curtain rod or dowel, and some fabric might work well to divide a large area. You could even hang beads if it works with the theme.

Prevent wasting time and energy moving heavy items back and forth by playing around with the layout of the space using a scaled floor plan and cutout furnishings. If you'd rather go the high-tech route, there are also a variety of CD-ROM products that will help with the layout. (See appendix B.)

The Webster (New York) Public Library opened the doors to its new young adult area in spring 2002. Working with an interior designer, the staff and its young adult advisors created a space with loads of teen appeal. The main focus

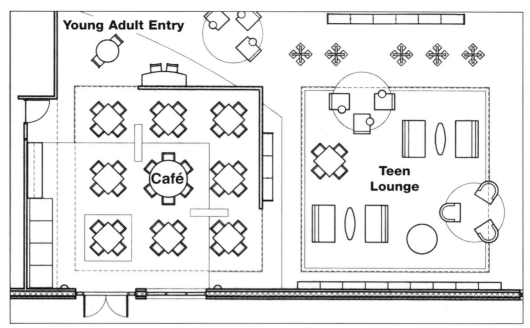

Furniture layout for the Webster (New York) Public Library young adult area

Architect s rendering of the teen lounge of the Webster (New York) Public Library
Credit: FJF Architects, LLP

of the space is a 1,200-square-foot lounging area located directly next to the café area (with vending machines) and adjacent to the computer center, audiovisual, young adult fiction, and adult/young adult nonfiction collections. The area is also within close distance of the service areas. The new design is just what teens ordered. (Previously, the area consisted of two aisles of books, two freestanding display units, wooden tables and chairs shared with the adult section, and a communal public access computer.) The new area consists of a suspended wire-mesh ceiling, little groupings of comfortable, up-to-date seating, a giant ottoman, a white board/bulletin board, tables for displays, and a huge, face-out magazine rack mounted to a sloping half wall that separates the café and the teen area. The half wall is wired for easy installation of additional PCs.

Space-Stretching Techniques

If you discover you're short on space once you begin laying out the area, try one of these helpful, space-stretching ideas.

Experiment by moving furnishings and fixtures around within the space and relocating unused items from other areas of the library.

Mount small display units at ends of shelves, the sides of bookcases, and on windows with suction cups.

Think vertical. Stack crates or cubes to create dimension and portable displays.

Use portable display units on casters for magazines and literature displays.

Use wall space to its maximum potential. For example, if you can't find room for a bulletin board, adhere cork tiles between shelves or create a freestanding board that can be moved around the room.

Use the ceiling as much as possible by suspending three-dimensional objects, art, and posters from it. For two-dimensional objects such as posters: cut a piece of foam core to match the size, mount the images on both sides of the foam, and suspend the foam from the ceiling with the appropriate weight fishing line. The same principle applies to three-dimensional objects: attach the fishing line to the object and suspend it from the ceiling with hooks.

Weed the collection to make space for new items (but also go into the children's area and make sure teen-appropriate materials aren't hiding there).

Finally, when it comes to layout (or any of the areas discussed in this chapter), if you can't afford to hire a professional, try forming a young adult space makeover club. Get together with a group of librarians in your area who have a situation similar to yours and set up a series of visits to each person's library. During visits, experiment with ideas, move things around, and brainstorm for the future. Generate more-extensive decorating projects that each librarian (and teen helpers) can work on after the initial visit.

Naming and Signage

Over the last several years, there has been much discussion about naming library spaces for young adults. Areas labeled Young Adult, YA, and Teens have all been criticized at one time or another. Some have suggested not naming the area at all, and others have broken out of naming the area for the age group and started naming it as a place. So, what is a librarian to do?

First of all, don't worry about a "right" name and a "wrong" name because there is no such thing. Second of all, listen to what your teens have to say about the name for their area. From the moment the *Teen Spaces* advisory council members were polled, it was evident that the term "teens" was more appealing to the 12- to 14- year-olds than it was to the 15+ crowd. It was unanimous that all members hated the term "YA." In fact, most didn't have a clue about what "YA" meant. One 13-year-old girl asked, "Is that like YMCA without the *M* and the *C*?" (Bear in mind she didn't know what YMCA stood for either.) Although this comment was quite humorous to the group at the time, it is a very poignant commentary on how librarians classify teens. We refer to them and their materials with a term that they themselves do not understand. Knowing how teens feel about the term, why do librarians continue using this acronym? (Notice that the term "YA" is used as little as possible in this book.)

To make your library a true teen haven, it's important that you take their comments seriously. It appears that teenagers are telling us we're making a huge marketing blunder by promoting a service with a term the customer can't identify with. To remedy this problem, teens tell us to get rid of "YA" and come up with something clearly identifiable, something universal, something *better.*

The best solution to naming a library space for teens is to have teens name it themselves. Hold a contest or vote on the name at a teen advisory meeting, but whatever you do, don't try to come up with something on your own—it will surely backfire. Many times adults assume a name is "hip" when, in actuality, it isn't. The key here is not to waste time, effort, and money on a sign that will turn teens away faster than you can get them in. Libraries across the United States have chosen names based on teen input, and it works. In fact, it's how most of the model libraries came up with or will be determining the phrasing for their new spaces.

The *Teen Spaces* advisory council came up with a few naming guidelines. They suggested that the name of a young adult space *should* be

  inconspicuous

  short and to the point

  catchy

  something that goes with the decoration and theme of the space

Following is a sampling of what they said the space should *not* be called:

  It should not contain the word "center."

  The term YA should not be used.

  The label should not sound too set up (i.e., "The Hangout").

  Anything corny or childish (i.e., "The Rad Bad Teen Center") is not good.

TIP

Listen to what your teens have to say about the name for their area. To make your library a true teen haven, it's important that you take their comments seriously.

"The Young Adult Area" shouldn't be used.

Do not use anything alliterative.

Avoid a "play on words" (i.e., "The Pitt Stop" in Pittsford Place).

Intentional misspellings are generally not cute (i.e., "The Korner").

Do not use anything long.

The Physical Sign

For the actual design of teen area signage, once again, stay away from those trendy elements that would be permanent and difficult to modify. If for some

Sign for teen area in Lawrence (Kansas) Public Library

reason a trendy name is a must for your library, make sure that the sign can be changed easily when the name goes out of style. In this situation, something painted on the wall would work well. An interchangeable sign (one where the letters slide in and out) would also work well. More permanent options include custom-made architectural, screen-printed, neon, and backlit signs or a programmable motion message display. See the Swampscott (Massachusetts) Public Library and Schaumburg (Illinois) Township District Library signs shown earlier in this chapter and the Lawrence (Kansas) Public Library for three excellent and quite diverse examples of attention-grabbing young adult signs.

Miscellaneous Signage

Any sign displayed in a teen area—whether the name of the space, Dewey Decimal guides, or signs depicting the various collections—needs to be large, interesting, and eye-catching. When making or purchasing signs of any kind, keep them simple and interesting. Be bold, not boring. Bad signage can quickly ruin any library space, especially when it's drab, too small, and inappropriate for teens. It's especially distressing to see a beautiful teen area with great potential spoiled by disproportionate signage.

You can make signs on the computer and print them in colors that are bright and that coordinate with the space. Use fonts that are easy to read, yet fun. Incorporate letters cut out from an Ellison machine for something different. Overlap the letters or cut them out of interesting paper. Then laminate the signs to give them durability and a professional look. (Contact paper will work if you don't have a laminator.) If your budget allows, incorporate a white board or a chalkboard into the mix. In addition to a neon sign that designates its teen area as "Teen Café Read," the Chicago Ridge (Illinois) Library incorporated a black wet-erase board with attached corkboard and titled it "Teen Happenings" to draw attention to new materials and upcoming events.

Think about different ways to display signs and posters such as suspending them with fishing line from the ceiling, presenting them in acrylic sleeves of varying sizes, and mounting things in unusual places such as adhering them directly to the ceiling or having them stick out from shelving ranges. Another innovative idea is to use alternative wording for "everyday" signs. For example, Phoenix Public Library identifies fiction as "A Good Read" and nonfiction as "Info." Browse through teen magazines and video catalogs to get more ideas like this. Be careful of using words that are out-of-date. Today's word for "cool" is tomorrow's word for "out-of-date" (i.e., "awesome" in the 1980s, "phat" in the 1990s, and "hot" in 2001). However, no matter what the other signs say, remember the most important sign is the one that says, "These items can be checked out."

The key to successfully designing and decorating the ideal teen area is to start with a fresh eye and an open mind. Be creative, whether it's with the walls, ceiling, layout, or signage. Avoid falling into the trap of that's how we've always done it but, instead, use color, texture, lighting, furniture, and accessories to break free from the mold. Success will come to those who aren't afraid to think outside the box, who frequently consult teen advisors, and actively seek advice from professionals and retailers outside the library world.

Notes

1. Information submitted by Bonnie Grimble, School Media Department Chair (Carmel High School, Carmel, Ind., 2001).
2. Taken in part from "Designing a School Library," *School Libraries in Canada* 19, no. 3 (1999): 18–21.
3. Taken in part from the American Society of Interior Designers, Working with an Interior Designer. Available www.asid.org (8 Sept. 2001).
4. Suggested by Amy Alessio, the teen coordinator for the Schaumburg (Illinois) Township District Library in cooperation with the Chicago Design Company during the renovation of the library's teen area in February/March 2001.
5. Anthony Bernier, "On My Mind: Young Adult Spaces," *American Libraries* 29, no. 9 (Oct. 1998): 52.
6. Ideas taken in part from the Phoenix (Arizona) Public Library's design and create meetings, 2000–2001.
7. Sally Cochran and Peter Gisolfi, "Renovate It and They Will Come: Designing a Popular High School Library," *School Library Journal* 43, no. 2 (Feb. 1997): 25–9. Taken in part from Peter Gisolfi (Peter Gisolfi Associates, Hastings-on-Hudson, N.Y.) who worked with library media specialist Sally Cochran in 1995–1996 to renovate the Horace Greeley High School in Chappaqua, N.Y.
8. Vicky M. Pratt, "Going a Long Way on a Short Budget," *Voices of Youth Advocates* 24, no. 4 (Oct. 2001): 264–5.
9. Wanda Higgins, "What Do Young Adults Want in Their School Library?" *Book Report* 18, no. 2 (Sept./Oct. 1999): 25–7.
10. The *Teen Spaces* advisory council members were periodically surveyed throughout 2001. Information from the Phoenix (Arizona) Public Library was gathered from written surveys as well as directly from teens at a series of five focus group meetings held between June 2000 and August 2000. Findings submitted by Carol Finch, youth services coordinator.

5 Long-Term Promotion

After you've created the ideal young adult space, how do you get teens to use it? If teens were involved in the planning and design process of the space, then you are off to a good start. Getting teens involved at the beginning will lead to enthusiasm and excitement. Before you know it, more and more teens will find out what's happening at the library with little effort on your part. However, after the initial excitement, how do you keep them coming back? You must consider your long-term promotion of teen spaces and services and ways to generate fresh ideas to keep teens interested long after the ribbon has been cut.

Keeping a library filled with teenagers is not as difficult as one might think. The key is to let them know about the new space, materials, programs, and services available to them. Most importantly, let them know they are welcome. Effective collection development and inventive programming coupled with creative merchandising and advertising, strong public relations, and active teen involvement are all necessary elements for making a young adult space thrive in the short term and in the long run.

Adults and the Teen Area

The first step in packing a library with teenagers is, by far and wide, having "cool" staff. According to the *Teen Spaces* advisory council, being able to relate to and talk to an adult is high on their list. Teens are more likely to visit the library and use its services if they like and feel comfortable with the people working there. When asked, "What types of people would you absolutely hate to see in a teen area?" they responded:

mean, grumpy people

people who look stern and old fashioned

someone who always watches you

people who make you feel stupid

When asked, "What kind of people should be working in a teen area?" they said:

adults who like to work with us

friendly people who come up to you

someone you can talk to

enthusiastic people

fun people with cool ideas

overall cool people that are easy to get along with

people with good looks

college students and teens

Teens today are very visual people and have been raised on pop culture, so it is only natural for them to respond like this. It's essential that teens see the new image of librarians. Regarding this image, Tyrone Ward, a manager at a west side branch of the Chicago Public Library, was quoted as saying, "The school-marmish librarian, with the reading glasses and the long dress and the bun in her hair, was a wonderful lady, very loving and very devoted to her work, but her day is gone. The stereotype has more life than she does."[1] Even in the age of computers, there is no substitute for the "human touch"—a touch that comes from someone who is fun, smart, and full of style.

Another issue related to adults and teens is that of adult library patrons using the teen area. It has been an issue for years and is a common occurrence in most public libraries. Adults seem to find their way to the young adult area time after time. If a teen area is empty, no matter how new it is, adults will eventually find their way there because, to them, an empty area, no matter whom it's designated for, is a quiet place to think and read. The issue here is not a question of adults using teen areas; it is a problem of teens underusing libraries, in particular, their space. By creating a place that is especially designed for teens, something that screams "teenager" both visually and emotionally, you will surely keep adult patrons in their own area of the library.

The Right Materials

A winning young adult collection is another strong asset of a teen space. The recipe for success is to start with tons of great teen materials and an array of computers and other technologies, then insert some creative marketing and merchandising.

The Collection

The two elements that make a young adult collection truly unbeatable are content and appearance. Pack your library's new space with items that teens want such as

- an extensive magazine collection
- paperback fiction
- graphic novels

- a wide selection of audiovisual items: videos, DVDs, books on cassette and CD, CD-ROMs, music CDs
- a strong nonfiction collection that includes a variety of topics that are curriculum-based as well as popular (things teens want to read about for pleasure)
- well-defined special collections

  a strong college collection including college catalogs, exam preparation guides, and college handbooks

  a "required reading" collection featuring curriculum-related items that students must read during the school year and during the summer

  either a circulating or reference-only games collection of both the board and video variety

  a careers section that includes helpful resources for older teens such as job-hunting materials and books on writing résumés and interviewing skills (Even though careers collections commonly reside in the adult section of most public libraries, consider locating them in an area near the young adult area. If relocation is not possible, make sure the collection is prominently advertised somewhere in the young adult area so teens know it is available to them.)

A first-rate young adult collection also means frequent and generous weeding. Materials must be current. Active weeding not only ensures an up-to-date collection, it makes room for new purchases as well as for marketing new materials. Outdated content and cover art can be fatal to teen services. Items that are housed in a new teen space should be exciting and attractive. The wider the variety of formats the better. Publicize the collection by creating lists of helpful resources around the library and posting them on the Web. For example, Berkeley (California) Public Library found that this practice increased the odds of attracting teens by showing them that the library is in tune with topics that are of high interest to people their age.[2] Creating a materials selection committee is an excellent way to give teens a sense of ownership and connection to the library while ensuring that the materials purchased for the library are what they want. This group could stem from a teen advisory board or exist as a completely separate entity. General guidelines include the following:

Involve as wide a variety of teens as possible, ages 12 to 18. Keep the group to between 10 and 15 participants or else it becomes unwieldy.

Distribute lists and reviews of potential purchases to participants at the first meeting.

Meet once a month for approximately 1 to 1-1/2 hours to review materials.

Choose a different media type each month to provide focus to the group and to prevent overwhelming participants. Consider creating a monthly schedule, for example, January, April, August for fiction books; February, May, September for videos and DVDs; March, October for books on cassette or CD; June, November for CD-ROMs; July, December for graphic novels.

Create informational packets for participants. At the end of each meeting, hand out a list of items to be considered for the following meeting. Consult *School Library Journal, Booklist,* and other relevant journals to assist in the selection process. For alternative formats look to

music: *Billboard, Entertainment Weekly, Rolling Stone*

books on cassette and CD: standard library journals such as *Booklist* but also vendor catalogs from Audio Editions, Books on Tape, Brilliance, Listening Library, and Recorded Books, etc.

videos/DVDs: *Booklist, Library Journal, Video Librarian,* and vendor catalogs from Midwest Tape, Library Video, Instructional Video, Critics' Choice Video, and Baker & Taylor Entertainment

Amazon.com

At each meeting, ask teens to present their reviews and ideas, and have them vote on each item. Whichever items get the most votes are the ones to purchase. As a reward, give the committee members first chance to check out materials they selected. Design special labels or bookmarks for the items so that other teens will know that the items were selected by their peers.

Technology

Technology is "hot" with teens; it's part of their lives. Therefore it must play a large part in any young adult space. Consider a young adult space filled with listening stations, a big screen TV equipped with a VCR and DVD player, and computers with access to the online catalog, the Internet, electronic games, research databases, and software necessary for school work (i.e., MS Word, Excel, PowerPoint, etc). A strong collection of paper, electronic, and audiovisual resources is important, as is the technology that goes along with the resources—the machinery necessary to listen to music CDs, watch videos and DVDs, etc.

Incorporating technology into a teen space does not have to be an intimidating project. Start out small, and work your way up. For instance, start out with a 21-inch TV, a stereo, and a few pairs of headphones, and see what happens. The following year you might decide to introduce portable listening stations, a DVD player, and a Sony Playstation. See chapter 4 to see what libraries across the country are doing with technology, including two of the biggest movers and shakers in this area, the Phoenix Public Library and the Los Angeles Public Library.

If your library is small or medium-sized and the thought of setting up and maintaining technology of any kind is completely overwhelming, consider asking teens for assistance. Teenagers (a.k.a., teen tech assistants) are a great resource for setting up computers, hooking up TVs and VCRs, and maintaining equipment once it's in place. It's always better to seek help rather than do without simply because you do not have the knowledge or the time to go about it. Contact the middle or high school technology specialist to get names of potential volunteers. You might even have a teenaged page on staff who has a knack for computers and electronics.

One project you might want to consider is the installation of a "mini-network" in addition to your library's primary network. The computer setup in this project will not be connected to your library's local area network. A mini-network is an easy, inexpensive way to introduce technology without the hassle and expense. If new computers are out of the question, consider purchasing recycled ones or see if the library has any older models that can be upgraded and reused. Also, try to use computers equipped with CD-ROM drives so the workstations can double as listening stations. To create a two to four workstation network you will need

two to four computers

four-port hub

network cables

a printer (and its software)

an easy-to-use desktop security program such as *Fortres*

desired software

Include entertainment and educational programs such as games, MS Office, etc. Try to be consistent with standard word processing software. Find out what the local middle and high schools are using if you're in a public library environment.

A mini-network is generally a means for teens to work on homework, write letters, listen to music, etc., within the confines of the teen area. In most instances, it will not include Internet access if there is means for access elsewhere in the library, although it could be an option if there is a phone jack nearby and dial-up access is in the budget.

Programming

Creative and appealing teen programs are a vital component of any young adult space. Aside from the recreational function, programs can also function as a type of promotional tool by providing a means of attracting teens to the library. Once teens are at the library, this gives you the opportunity to showcase what you have to offer them. Those with a solid young adult programming plan who are dedicated to seeing it through are the ones who are the most successful in attracting teens to their libraries. When developing a programming plan, keep in mind that a variety of types and levels of activities is necessary to meet the diverse needs and interests of adolescents. In addition, just as it was important to involve teens in the planning and implementation of their new space, it is equally important to include them in programming once the space is finished.

It is beyond the scope of this book to go into detail about programming for teens. However, following are some inventive ideas to help spark creativity and assist in encouraging teens to come to the library's

TIP

Just as it was important to involve teens in the planning and implementation of their new space, it is equally important to include them in programming once the space is finished.

TIP

Find out directly
from teens what
types of programs
they'd like to see
at the library.

newly designed young adult area. When creating a programming list for teens, always keep in mind teen interests. What do they most like to do? What is "hot" at the moment? Figure 5.1 is a sample list of programs based on top teen activities.

Find out directly from teens what types of programs they'd like to see at the library. The *Teen Spaces* advisory council suggested the following ideas:

an after-school study hall where teens can get help from teachers or from National Honor Society students (Note that this would provide a teen volunteer opportunity as well as a wonderful service.)

FIGURE 5.1
Program Ideas Based on Teen Interests

Top Teen Leisure-Time Activities	Program Ideas
Watching TV or movies	Monthly movie screenings Series of workshops on making a music video
Listening to the radio, CDs, or tapes	Teen bands in the park Win your favorite CD contest
Hanging out with friends	Media discussion (reviews of movies, graphic novels, or music)
Talking on the phone	Junior Friends of the Library (fundraising assistants)
Reading magazines and newspapers	Magazine and comic book exchange Teen library newsletter
Exercising or playing sports	Dances Interactive demonstrations of popular activities, such as soccer
Cooking	Cooking classes of quick and easy snacks, etc. Taste-off of teen-made pizzas
Using a computer	Teen web committee Computer classes in which teens teach senior citizens Computer game contests
Reading books for pleasure	Book discussion groups Online book review committees
Shopping or going to the mall	Buying trips for materials or design/decorating items for teen space

Source: "Top Teen Leisure Activities" based on Peter Zollo's *Wise Up to Teens: Insights into Marketing and Advertising to Teenagers* (Ithaca, New York: New Strategist Publications, 1999).

board game or computer game tournaments

movie screenings

group study sessions

an anniversary celebration of the opening of the teen space or the opening of the library as a whole

anything with food, drink, and talking

a library "how-to" program offered yearly that would include a tour of the library, where and how to access the Internet, and other technologies and services available (reference assistance, copying machine, printers, scanners, etc.) and would highlight special collections and point out things teens might not know are available to them such as videos, DVDs, graphic novels, music, and college and careers information

For more ideas to fuel your imagination, refer to the various editions of Mary K. Chelton's *Excellence in Library Services to Young Adults: The Nation's Top Programs* and *Youth Participation in School and Public Libraries: It Works* by Caroline Caywood.[3]

For general programming assistance, refer to books such as Patrick Jones's *Connecting Young Adults and Libraries* or Mary Anne and C. Allen Nichols's *Young Adults and Public Libraries*.[4] Check with your state library system for local programming publications such as the New York Library Association's *The Basic Young Adult Services Handbook: A Programming and Training Manual*. (See appendix B.) Journals such as *Voice of Youth Advocates* and *Journal of Youth Services and Libraries,* youth-related discussion lists such as PUBYAC and YA-YAAC, and individual library web pages are also good resources for programming ideas.

Once you have a solid list of programming ideas, start involving teens. Get their thoughts on the topics. What are potential "winners" and "losers"? Do they have ideas for speakers/presenters? Brainstorm creative ways to advertise and promote the events because the key here is to intrigue them enough to get them in and, once they're there—amaze them, "wow" them, keep them coming back for more.

Marketing and Merchandising

Marketing is all about reaching the customer—hearing what young people have to say, understanding what they need and want, and learning how to incorporate that information into the products or services provided. In today's world, there are no limits to what can be marketed, including food, technology, fashion, entertainment, and, yes, even the library. Public and school libraries are ripe for marketing to teens. Where else can teenagers find an array of entertainment choices, reliable homework assistance, free computer use, and their friends all rolled up in one? There is definitely potential for major teen appeal here. The key is in learning how to figure out what teens want and how to connect that information with what libraries are "selling."

Marketing makes it all work. Just take a look at successful companies that cater to teens such as Nike, Gap, and Pepsi. Businesses such as these are the marketing experts, and libraries could learn a lot from them when it comes to advertising and retailing. After all, teenagers spend more than $100 billion every year on these businesses.[5] Businesses with successful marketing targeted to teens know exactly how to tie in a teenager's wants with their companies products. Therefore, don't waste time reinventing the wheel. Make some observations and do a little research. A wealth of wonderful resources are out there dealing specifically with marketing to teens. Peter Zollo's *Wise Up to Teens: Insights into Marketing and Advertising to Teenagers* and Elissa Moses's *The $100 Billion Allowance* are two of the best. As Moses points out, there are twelve steps to successful marketing to teens:

1. dream	7. get the big picture
2. reality check	8. ladder your assets
3. take stock	9. create your own luck
4. do research	10. fine-tune your target
5. get organized	11. assess the differentiators
6. profile your prime prospect	12. be real and respectful[6]

Visual Merchandising

TIP

Merchandising is a great interactive, ongoing project for members of a teen advisory board or teen library pages.

The retail term *visual merchandising* means making materials eye-catching, attractive, and exciting by effectively displaying them for the customer. It's all about placing the right materials in the right formats in the right spots.[7] When done correctly, merchandising serves two purposes: It makes the customer stop and look, and it assists in creating visual stimulus, functioning as part of the "décor" of the space. In fact, how the collection is presented and displayed will affect the entire look of the area. A library's ultimate merchandising goal is to effectively present materials as a means to increase circulation by getting books, videos, magazines, and music off the shelves and into a patron's hands. Merchandising is a great interactive, ongoing project for members of a teen advisory board or teen library pages. Schedule different teens or teams of teens to be in charge of promoting the collection each month. What a terrific way to familiarize them with the collection while actively involving them in maintaining the space. Following is a selected list of merchandising tools to consider for any teen area:

• literature racks	• bins
• slatwall panels	• pedestals
• spinner racks	• kiosks
• shelf talkers (small signs sticking out from shelves)	• props/3-D objects
• "dumps" (freestanding bin-like fixtures)	• bulletin boards
	• zigzag shelves
• showcases	• sign holders
• milk crates	• freestanding display units
• slant shelves	• corner shelves

- book easels
- grid shelving
- signs
- wall pockets

- cubes
- folding screens
- cork rails and cork panels

Successful, attention-grabbing displays can be done at little to no cost, in a relatively small amount of time, and with very little effort. Add interest and visual stimulation by introducing exciting displays using books, videos, brochures, or whatever you think works.

One of the simplest and most effective ways to display materials is to highlight items using face-out merchandising in which the cover is showing. This can be done pretty much anywhere, but one of the most popular places is at the ends of shelves. Make sure each shelf has ample room for face-out display, and if it doesn't, rearrange the shelves or weed to make room. Never be skimpy with face-out merchandising. Cover artwork is the key to circulation success, especially where hardcover fiction books are concerned. Keep in mind that a cover with exciting artwork is always a better enticement than a boring spine.

Another resourceful way to create effective displays while adding interest to a teen space is to use nonstandard shelving that has built-in display potential. Products include bookstore-style slant or zigzag shelves, slatwall units, milk crates, stackable wooden cubes, wall mounted grid racks, or other systems similar to those seen in a video store or retail space. Other types of displays would include end-of-the-range units and freestanding displays. Both can be created using readymade display racks or existing furniture such as tables, blocks, etc.

When it comes to teen spaces, it's important to never waste space. The same holds true for displays. Look around at the spots that aren't being used but that have potential to make an impact. A few space saving items to consider for purchase or in-house creation include end-of-the range shelving, mobile display units, freestanding shelving such as spinner racks and gondolas (island displays), wall pockets for magazines and literature, window display units (mounted with suction cups), and folding screens that can double as a room divider and a resourceful merchandising tool.

Face-out display and comfortable atmosphere in an alcove of the Allen County Public Library (Fort Wayne, Indiana)

The key to success with freestanding displays is locating them in high traffic areas—anywhere they'll be noticed. Encourage point-of-purchase (P.O.P.) displays located near key service areas such as reference or circulation. An alternative location for a P.O.P. display would be somewhere near the front of the library. This would grab the attention of those teens actively avoiding service areas. If you're in a multiple-story library, stock a display of new materials on the first floor to encourage teens to visit upstairs. In the business world, the P.O.P. advertising industry is a $12 billion

Freestanding slatwall kiosk display and a student art exhibit in teen area at the Peabody (Massachusetts) Institute Library

a year business and still growing, so it must be doing something right.[8] P.O.P. displays are great for highlighting "hot" items, encouraging impulse "buying," and for showing teens something they might not have otherwise seen. Such displays can be created with counter display units, book dumps, or tabletop displays. Standard library counter units come in many sizes and are generally made of cardboard, wire, wood, or acrylic. Book dumps also come in a variety of sizes and styles and are extremely versatile. Simply throw materials in, pile them up, and let teens pick through them.

No matter what type of display you're creating or how and where you choose to build it, there are a few basic rules for ensuring display success:

Use gimmicks that get attention.

Introduce "visual variety" by incorporating three-dimensional objects that complement the theme of the display.

Present the materials with the covers face out.

Incorporate signage that is eye-catching, easy to follow, and on target with the theme to direct teens to specific collections.

Scan and replenish displays frequently (about once a week) to keep things looking fresh and exciting as well as to get an idea of what's moving and what's not.

Finally, remember that fabulous doesn't have to equal expensive. See the photos from Mercer County's Lawrence Headquarters (Lawrenceville, New Jersey) for some artistic and inventive examples. Inexpensive book easels are one of the best merchandising investments you could make, and they can be used almost anywhere to display

Magnetic spinner for program advertising used at Mercer County's Lawrence Headquarters (Lawrenceville, New Jersey)

Attention-grabbing displays and funhouse mirror on the wall in the center of the display at Mercer County's Lawrence Headquarters

materials or signs. Shelf talkers are another great, low-cost way to quickly attract attention. Retail stores regularly use them to highlight items and provide information. Get creative with labels and signage because they too will go a long way for little money.

Bookstore Basics

Over the past several years there has been a great interest in modeling libraries after bookstores. Bookstores are successful primarily because they know how to entice their customers with effective marketing. Libraries are behind the times in promoting their products and services to the public, and to teens in particular, and competition from bookstores is fierce. In a bookstore teens can wander, browse by familiar topics, and freely eat, drink, and socialize. In a library teens are faced with the mystifying Dewey Decimal system, forbidden to eat and drink, and regularly reprimanded for socializing. Given that information, where would you choose to hang out?

The first thing we can learn from bookstores is the power of browsing. The way libraries organize materials can be intimidating to users, especially those with short attention spans or those unfamiliar with library classification rules. Featuring items by subject and highlighting teen-related materials is an essential part of making teens feel comfortable in a bookstore.

Bookstores are also good resources for signage and for labels in browsing areas. You can insert attractive, clearly labeled signage either projecting from or hanging above the nonfiction stacks. This is a simple and effective way to show patrons where key subject areas begin.

Another great way to improve access to a library's teen fiction collection is to create genre lists. Generate recommended reading lists or viewing lists called "rave reviews" or "hot picks" using resources such as *What Do Young Adults Read Next?*, Betty Carter's *Best Books for Young Adults,* or *Selected Videos and DVDs for Young Adults.*[9] See Patrick Jones's *Connecting Young Adults and Libraries* for more suggestions. How about purchasing readymade pamphlets such as "Top 100 Books for Teens" or "Outstanding Books for the College Bound?" Contact YALSA for more information on brochures and pamphlets.

Including genre labels on materials is another easy way to improve access to the collection. Look through catalogs to find labels that coordinate with the genre lists. (See appendix B for a list of suggested suppliers.) Video store catalogs are great resources for creative label ideas. If you don't like the readymade labels or can't find all the categories you need, make them yourself. Create stickers using Microsoft Publisher, Printshop, or even Microsoft Word, and print them on Avery Labels (size 5262). Enlarge the labels and print them as signs to advertise and as a handy resource for staff and teens.[10] Then, once you have your teens' attention and they feel at ease, work on teaching them the Dewey Decimal system.

Teens gravitate to bookstores because they can hang out and relax. Being able to find materials easily, eat, talk, and listen to music plays a large part in the comfort zone of teens, so being in a bookstore is *almost* like being home. If teens feel more "at home" at the library, it's more likely that they will want to hang out there. We say that we want teens to use the library, but we contradict ourselves by establishing rules that prohibit eating chips and drinking a soda. All of the teens in the *Teen Spaces* advisory council said that they need comfort, snacks, and background music when studying. Therefore, this book stresses comfortable, cozy seating rather than traditional library furnishings, increased technology, and consideration of library policies on eating, playing music, and talking.

In essence, libraries should take a serious look at bookstores and other retailers providing service to teens. However, even though bookstores do a great job, libraries could do it better.

Advertising

One way to effectively get the word out to teens about your new teen space and programs is through effective advertising. Advertisements come in the form of various media types including television, magazines, radio, movie ads, posters, billboards, newspapers, mail, and the Internet, to name just a few. The common thread that links each of these formats is *content*. To be successful in advertising, it is imperative that the content of the ad be exciting and appeal to its intended audiences. Ads geared toward teens must be created just for them—not for children under age 12, parents, or any adults. According to teen marketing expert Elissa Moses, there is only one cardinal rule of advertising that is especially true when targeting teens: "Thou shalt not be boring!"[11] Following are her top ten types of advertising that appeal to teens:

- Make me laugh.
- Be fun.
- Use popular music.
- Be realistic.
- Use young actors.
- Use contemporary colors and graphics.
- Use special effects.
- Show the product.
- Tell an interesting story.
- Show the "company" cares.[12]

Knowing that exciting and appealing are musts, take a look at print advertising. People of all ages are bombarded with printed materials every day, so much, in fact, that this type of advertising is generally ignored. Therefore, it is crucial that print advertising be creative. Posters—the larger the better—are great tools, as are advertisements in the school newspaper. Several of the older members of the *Teen Spaces* advisory council suggested posting library information in the local paper next to the police beat because they said all teens look there. Teen newsletters are also gaining popularity in paper as well as online. Bulk mailings of a teen newsletter are a great way to reach both library users and nonusers. An electronic newsletter can be a great advertising and public relations tool for a public or school library. It is also an excellent interactive, skill-building project for teen volunteers. Include photographs, drawings, stories, "top ten" lists, program information, teen reviews, editorials, an advice column, or whatever comes to mind. For example, the Garfield Park Branch, Santa Cruz (California) Public Libraries, has done just that. Their teen advisory council has created an online newsletter called *What's Next?* (See appendix C.)

No matter what you choose to do, get teens' attention by making materials simple, attention grabbing, and visually stimulating. Following are twenty-five promotional and public relations ideas for marketing library services to young adults. Many of these could be developed by teens.

1. Stuff fliers into related books on a thematic display in the library.
2. Mail a newsletter or flier to past participants in programs. (Keep your attendance logs or registration sign-up sheets.)
3. Send fliers or posters to other neighboring libraries.
4. For writing contests, keep a binder of entries and winners on display in the teen area throughout the year.
5. Distribute program fliers in the local hangouts and schools.
6. Hang posters at related businesses (e.g., at a comicbook store for a graphic novels workshop).
7. Put program fliers at the businesses that have sponsored incentive prizes for library programs or given funds to underwrite programs.
8. Submit an article to the arts council or other community agencies.
9. Set up an interview for yourself and teen supporters and promote the teen center and related programs on the radio, television, and the web.
10. Call teens directly to invite them to participate.
11. Hang posters in schools, the mall, and favorite teen hangouts and eating places.
12. Personally recruit regular library users.
13. Get referrals from young adult advisory council members.
14. Send newsletters or direct mailings to youth groups.
15. Send articles to locally produced magazines for teens and school newspapers.
16. Work out a deal with your local cable television station to produce commercials advertising the teen center and its services.
17. Have a booth at the summer information fair, community fair, etc.
18. Set up point-of-purchase displays with materials and fliers at key services areas.
19. Submit an article for the local recreation department's newsletter.
20. Place a paid ad in the local paper. Make it look like a retail advertisement.
21. For contests, display the winning entries at schools or, if it is a school library contest, display them at the public library.
22. Make classroom visits.
23. Have teens read announcements on the public address system at school or on the school radio station.
24. Set up a display in the showcase at local schools.

25. Create online surveys or distribute paper surveys to teens asking what they want at their library. Incorporate questions in such a way that the survey functions as an informational tool, letting teens know what's at the library and what they've been missing.

Once the promotional materials are produced, take time to think about strategic locations. Post fliers and posters in creative, attention-grabbing places including school, the school newspaper, and local teen hangouts such as movie theaters, clubs, community centers, arcades, and coffee shops. If you haven't already done so, this is the time to partner with local teen-related groups as well as to cultivate the valuable school/public library relationship.

Alternative media such as TV, radio, and the Internet are also great ways to capture the attention of teens. Most teens name cable TV, magazines, and radio as the advertising media to which they pay the most attention.[13] Television advertising may seem prohibitive because of the cost, but check with your local television station to see if you can work out a deal. For example, the Saginaw (Michigan) Public Libraries got their message out using cable television, radio, and newspaper ads, and they involved teens in the process by having them help create and sometimes act in the ads. Contact the Saginaw Public Libraries for more information. (See appendix C). A less-expensive and highly effective advertising alternative is online advertising as long as it is done in conjunction with web sites that are frequently visited by teens. (See appendix B.)

Another marketing alternative is to put together an interactive CD-ROM that could be mailed or handed out to teens. Macy's sent out its first interactive CD-ROM to 500,000 teenagers in the summer of 2001. It included trends for the season, clips from movies and music, store event information, and a $5 gift card. Users could click on fashions worn by models to find out the price and brand. Libraries could definitely adapt this technique to highlight their products and services. The library's disc could include interactive information about the library; teen reviews of products and services; teen-created animated clips, games, art; homework help; and links to a variety of resources. You could even attach some type of incentive, such as a gift certificate or an entry for a prize drawing. The costs for something like this include $1,000 for software to create the CD-ROM (Macromedia Director is a good example), anywhere from $150 to $500 for a CD burner, and blank CD media (bundles of 50 are available for about $30). If this is too overwhelming for your staff and resources, try the coupon idea on its own. Creative paper advertising can be just as effective as multimedia promotion if it's done right.

Whether advertising in print or online, look toward successful teen web pages to see what actually attracts teens. (For a list of popular teen web sites, refer to appendix B.) Web pages such as these are also excellent inspirational resources for ideas for your teen space. The rules for creating a successful teen area and a successful teen web page are the same: know the customer, address functionality, plan, incorporate visual appeal, concentrate on interactivity, and keep it fresh and interesting. When designing a teen page keep in mind these basic principles:

Include the most important information in the first half of the screen because most teens do not like to scroll.

TIP

Involve teens
in the planning,
design, and
maintenance
of the web
page.

Keep it clear, organized, and simple.

Use graphic design as a means of enhancing communication with teens as well as for decoration

Consider reading patterns because any design that works in opposition to the way a teen reads interrupts the flow.

Create a focal point for the page. Generally, this is one-third down the page and slightly to the right of center. This is the best place for important information.

Choose words appropriate for teens, and keep sentences simple and to the point.

Use contrast (dark versus light) to create visual excitement. Dark areas draw attention. Use tone and contrast sparingly for the greatest impact.

Invite teens to look at your page by using pictures. Pictures should supplement the text around them, not serve as barriers.

Focus on interactivity by including links to interactive web pages or creating polls or online surveys.

Involve teens in the planning, design, and maintenance of the web page.[14]

Positive Public Relations

Positive public relations are a major component of effective marketing in teen services. Once a teenager has a negative experience, it generally sticks with him or her for a long time; therefore, it is important that libraries take a long, hard look at both the interaction of the staff with teens and the rules set forth by library administration. The goal is to have teens think affectionately about the library. You want them to feel comfortable with the space, the general atmosphere, and the staff. If they are not at ease, they will not stay.

Get Out of My Library . . .
But First, Could You Check out a Book?

How many times have teens been treated just like what's described in this heading?[15] We want teens to help us increase our statistics, yet we continually choose to treat them badly. Quite clearly, this attitude tells teens that we truly don't want their business. Many library workers admit that they want teens to use the library but that teen behavior and attention level drives them crazy; consequently, these workers are turned off to helping teens. Others struggle with being liked versus letting teens walk all over them. No doubt these are tough issues, but they're not as hopeless as you might think. Staff who are trained to understand the developmental needs and behaviors of teens are better able to cope and respond positively to difficult situations. It also needs to be clearly understood that customer service means consistently treating all patrons equally and with respect. Teens can recognize good service as quickly as anyone else, and it's this good service (and an occasional smile) that will keep them coming back.

In conjunction with staff interaction with teens, there's also the issue of library rules and regulations. The number one reason teens don't use libraries according to the *Teen Spaces* advisory council is because there are too many rules. As part of the process of increasing public relations, consider taking a long, hard look at the library rules that have a direct impact on teens, including age limits on computer use, restricted use of the Internet (no e-mail, no chatting, and no downloading), age limits on circulation of various material types (primarily audiovisual materials), eating and drinking in the library, and so on. Ask yourself, "Do the existing policies justifiably pertain to today's society and today's libraries?" The suggestion here is not to change everything, nor is it to question a rule that has legitimate validity, or to let teens run wild in the library. The challenge is simply to take an honest look at some of the regulations libraries have been carrying around for years and to see if they are appropriate for today's world. After all, it's not just teens who want to eat and drink in the library.

If you are still worried about spills and the noise level, here are some positive ideas that have worked for libraries across the country:

> The King County Public Library System in Washington has two of its branches stay open until midnight on Fridays so that teens have a safe place to hang out and keep off the streets.

> The Brooklyn Public Library opens the meeting room to teens once a week so they can have a place to eat, listen to music, watch TV, play games, and socialize without disturbing others.

> The Central Library of Jackson County Library Services in Medford, Oregon, schedules special Sunday hours for students to come learn how to conduct research and use library resources.[16]

Get the Word Out

Word-of-mouth is generally not considered an advertising medium because it is not a "controlled" format like print or television (i.e., it's not controlled because you don't have power over what is being said). Even though it's not considered a true advertising form, it is a fast and potentially effective way to promote and publicize teen services.

You must tell young adults what the library has to offer and show them it's a place that has people who genuinely relate to them and care about their needs. Effective promotion can be as simple as talking to teens who are using the library. Perhaps you have walked around and relocated teens working at "adult" tables or in the children's area to the young adult section. This is a wonderful opportunity for positive interaction and an extremely effective way of filling the new space and letting teens know what is available just for them.

Classroom visits are another excellent way for both public and school librarians alike to get the word out about teen services. Keep in mind that appearance and personality are very important to teens because this is your one chance to make a good first impression. (A bad first impression might be your last impression.) Keep classroom visits brief and interesting. As with advertising, it always helps to have a "gimmick" to get attention. After your initial connection, and when teens get to know you, they will pass the word along to others. There's no better publicity than positive peer-to-peer advertising. After all, teenagers are the primary source of information for teenagers, so get the word out and the rest will fall into place.

Whether designing a new teen area or trying to figure out how to sustain interest after the space is finished, it's essential to constantly keep in touch with the "consumer." Never stop asking yourself, "What do teens want, what do they need, and how do they use the library?" More importantly, never stop *asking teens* these same questions. Continue to involve teenagers in as many aspects of young adult services as possible because the ideal teen space will need continual support for it to remain the "ideal" teen space. Teens are the best partners you could have. They will be the ones who will be faithful about helping out and keeping bulletin boards, displays, posters, and collections up-to-date; they also will be the ones to draw in other teens. Simply remember the goal—to attract teens and keep them coming back often.

NOTES

1. John W. Fountain, "Librarians Adjust Image in an Effort to Fill Jobs," *New York Times* (23 Aug. 2001). (Online.)

2. For additional information see Regina Minudri, "The Top 10 Things You Need to Know about Teens," *School Library Journal* 45, no.1 (Jan. 1999): 30–1.

3. Mary K. Chelton, *Excellence in Library Services to Young Adults. The Nation's Top Programs,* 3d ed. (Chicago: American Library Assn., 2000); Caroline Caywood, *Youth Participation in School and Public Libraries: It Works* (Chicago: Young Adult Library Services Assn., 1995). The second edition of Chelton's book features the Pioneer Library System's (Canandaigua, New York) Young Adult Services for Generalists project.

4. Patrick Jones, *Connecting Young Adults and Libraries,* 2d ed. (New York: Neal Schuman, 1998); Mary Anne and C. Allen Nichols, *Young Adults and Public Libraries* (Westport, Conn.: Greenwood, 1998).

5. Elissa Moses, *The $100 Billion Allowance: Accessing the Global Teen Market* (New York: Wiley, 2000), 1–2.

6. Moses, 174–81.

7. Renée J. Vaillancourt, *Bare Bones Young Adult Services: Tips for Public Library Generalists* (Chicago: American Library Assn., 2000), 47.

8. Kimberly Bolan and Lisa C. Wemett, "Makeover Madness: Tips for Revamping Your Young Adult Area," *Voice of Youth Advocates* 22, no. 5 (December 1999): 322–3.

9. Idea of "Rave Reviews" borrowed from the Young Adult Librarians of Monroe County Library System, New York.

10. Idea taken in part from Laura Gruniger, Young Adult Librarian at the Mercer County Public Library, Lawrenceville, New Jersey.

11. Moses, 183.

12. Moses, 182. Used by permission of John Wiley & Sons, Inc.

13. Peter Zollo, *Wise Up to Teens: Insights into Marketing and Advertising to Teenagers* (Ithaca, N.Y.: New Strategist, 1999), 67.

14. Taken in part from Gail Junion-Metz, "Planning and Designing a Website for Kids and Teens" (New York State Library Association Workshop, 17 Oct. 2001, Albany, New York).

15. Heading and ideas derived from a young adult customer service training session held by Beth Kerrigan, young adult outreach librarian, Memorial Hall Library, Andover, Massachusetts, 24 Sept. 2001.

16. Joan Costello, Julie Spielberger, Sam Whalen, and Carolyn Winje, "Promoting Partnerships," *Journal of Youth Services in Libraries* 15, no. 1 (fall 2001): 11.

Worksheets

BRAINSTORMING IDEAS WORKSHEET

Service	Where have we been? (What are the library's current and past attitudes toward teens and young adult services?)	Where should we be? (How do young adult services relate to the library's mission, service priorities, long-range plan?)	Where are we headed? (Where would we like to see the library headed in regard to teens and young adult services?)
Target age range (grades 6–12 or grades 7–12)			
Scope of service (programs and special services)			
Collection (formats and budget)			
Technology (PCs, Internet, etc.)			
Staff and teens (customer service, staff time, teen stereotypes, behavior problems, etc.)			

Physical Space	Where have we been? (What are the library's current and past attitudes toward teens and young adult services?)	Where should we be? (How do young adult services relate to the library's mission, service priorities, long-range plan?)	Where are we headed? (Where would we like to see the library headed in regard to teens and young adult services?)
Location			
Function			
Content			
Layout			
Staffing			
Design			
Overall "feel" or "image"			

COMPARISON WORKSHEET

Library name _____ Date of comparison _____

	Entire Library Statistics	Children's Statistics	Adult Statistics	Young Adult Statistics	Proposed Young Adult Statistics
Service population					
Budget (include miscellaneous)					
Number of volumes					
Circulation					
Pecentage of total circulation		%	%	%	%
Books					
Magazines					
Audiovisual materials					
Online resources					
Other materials (list on back)					
Number of staff					
Program attendance (annual)					
Square footage					

SPACE NEEDS WORKSHEET

Note: Instructions for completing this worksheet as well as an Excel workbook based on this worksheet are available at http://www.dpi.state.wi.us/dlcl/pld/plspace.html.

Design Population

a. Current population of the municipality/primary service area _____

b. Projected population of the municipality/primary service area _____

c. Estimate of nonresident service population _____

d. Design population (b+c) _____

Step 1. Collection Space

a. Books   _____ volumes ÷ 10   _____ sq.ft.

b. Periodical (display)   _____ titles ÷ 1   _____ sq.ft.

c. Periodical (back issues)   _____ titles × 0.50 × _____ years retained   _____ sq.ft.

d. Nonprint   _____ items ÷ 10   _____ sq.ft.

e. Digital resources   _____ terminals × 50   _____ sq.ft.

f. Total (a + b + c + d + e)   _____ sq.ft.

Step 2. Reader Seating Space

a. _____ seats × 30   _____ sq.ft.

Step 3. Staff work space

a. _____ stations × 150 (list specific work stations on reverse)   _____ sq.ft.

Step 4. Meeting room space

a. General meeting space   _____ seats × 10 (plus 100 sq. ft. for speaker)   _____ sq.ft.

b. Conference room space   _____ seats × 25   _____ sq.ft.

c. Storytime space   _____ seats × 10 (plus 50 sq. ft. for speaker)   _____ sq.ft.

d. Total (a+b+c)   _____ sq.ft.

Step 5, Special use space

a. Collection space (from Step 1, item f)   _____ sq.ft.

b. Reader seating space (from Step 2, item a)   _____ sq.ft.

c. Staff work space (from Step 3, item a)   _____ sq.ft.

d. Meeting room space (from Step 4, item d)   _____ sq.ft.

e. **SUBTOTAL 1**   _____ sq.ft.

f. Divide subtotal 1 by 6 (for a minimum allocation), by 5 (for a moderate allocation), or by 4 (for an optimum allocation)   _____ sq.ft.

(Continued)

SPACE NEEDS WORKSHEET *(Continued)*

Step 6. Nonassignable space

a. Subtotal 1 (from Step 5, item e)   _____ sq.ft.

b. Special use space (from Step 5, item f)   _____ sq.ft.

c. **SUBTOTAL 2**   _____ sq.ft.

d. Divide Subtotal 2 by 4 (for a minimum allocation) or by 3
(for an optimum allocation)   _____ sq.ft.

Step 7. Putting it all together

a. Collection space (from Step 1, item f)   _____ sq.ft.

b. Reader seating space (from Step 2, item a)   _____ sq.ft.

c. Staff work space (from Step 3, item a)   _____ sq.ft.

d. Meeting room space (from Step 4, item d)   _____ sq.ft.

e. Special use space (from Step 5, item f)   _____ sq.ft.

f. Nonassignable space (from Step 6, item d)   _____ sq.ft.

g. **GROSS AREA NEEDED** (a + b + c + d + e + f)   _____ sq.ft.

Staff work stations
List here the staff work stations tallied and reported in Step 3:

_____

_____

_____

_____

_____

_____

_____

Notes:

_____

_____

_____

_____

_____

_____

_____

_____

TEEN SPACE PLANNING WORKSHEET

Action Step	Value	People	Money	Time

ACTION STEP BUDGET WORKSHEET

Action Step	Current Budget	Proposed Project Budget	Difference	Percent of Project Budget (Difference/ Total)	Notes
	$	$	$	%	
	$	$	$	%	
	$	$	$	%	
	$	$	$	%	
	$	$	$	%	
	$	$	$	%	
	$	$	$	%	
Total	$	$	$		

CATEGORIZED BUDGET WORKSHEET

Category	A. Current Budget	B. Proposed Project Budget	C. Additional Funds Needed to Complete Project (B – A)	D. Percent of Project Budget (C/Total C)	Notes
Architect/designer and consultant fees	$	$	$	%	
Furniture and fixtures	$	$	$	%	
Labor (remodeling, moving, etc.)	$	$	$	%	
Supplies (attach list)	$	$	$	%	
Rental equipment	$	$	$	%	
Technology	$	$	$	%	
Collection development	$	$	$	%	
Misc. long-term expense (i.e., additional staffing, telecommunications costs for Internet access)	$	$	$	%	
Publicity	$	$	$	%	
Total	$	$	$		

APPENDIX

B

Resources

Teen Interests and Involvement

Alloy
http://www.alloy.com
Cutting-edge style, news, and entertainment and "real life" information for teens. Includes advice boards, chat, and quizzes.

The Basic Young Adult Services Handbook: A Programming and Training Manual. Albany, New York: New York Library Assn., 1997.
Has more than 50 program listings including preparation steps, program content, and evaluation. Also includes information on the basics of young adult services, annotated bibliographies, training resources, and reproducible handouts for staff workshops or self-study.

Bassin, Ian, and Judy Goldberg. "From A to Z on the Net: The Purple Pages." *New York Times,* 24 April 2000, sec. A1.
"A guide to the most fun, useful, and thought-provoking Web sites for teens."

Carter, Betty, ed. *Best Books for Young Adults,* 2d ed. Chicago: American Library Assn., 2000.
Update to the 1994 release, this book is an essential resource for all teen librarians. It includes twenty-five bibliographies of best books as well as author-by-author, year-by-year, and topic-by-topic lists of exceptional books. For additional lists of best books, check out the YALSA web site at http://www.ala.org/yalsa/booklists/.

Caywood, Caroline. *Youth Participation in School and Public Libraries: It Works.* Chicago: American Library Assn., 1995.
Presents the rationales, directions, cautions, and support for youth participation programs.

Chelton, Mary K., ed. *Excellence in Library Services to Young Adults,* eds. 1–3. Chicago: American Library Assn., various dates.
All three editions present prizewinning programs that show teens as volunteers, employees, and mentors. Terrific resource for those interested in getting teens involved.

Friends of Libraries USA
1420 Walnut St, Ste. 450
Philadelphia, PA 19102-4017
800-9FOLUSA or 215-790-1674
http://www.folusa.com
Everything you need to know to help you start a Teen Friends group.

GamePro: World's Largest Multiplatform Gaming Magazine
IDG Communications Inc.
501 Second St., Ste. 500
San Francisco, CA 94107
http://gamepro.com
Just one of the many teen magazines on the market today. (Other magazines with teen appeal include *Billboard, Entertainment Weekly, Glamour, J-14, New Moon, People, Sports Illustrated, Right On, Rolling Stone, Seventeen, Teen People, Thrasher,*

TransWorld Skateboarding, Vibe, Vogue, WWF [World Wrestling Federation].) *GamePro's* emphasis is on PlayStation, Nintendo 64, and Dreamcast electronic game systems with information on the newest games and best tips. Evaluates every game for graphics, sound, control, and "fun factor."

Higgins, Wanda. "What Do Young Adults Want in Their School Library?" *Book Report* 18, no.2 (Sept./Oct. 1999): 25–7.

Useful for getting a quick overview of what teens need and want in their school library media center.

Jones, Patrick. *Connecting Young Adults and Libraries: A How-to-Do-It Manual,* 2d ed. New York: Neal-Schuman, 1998.

Chock full of information on teens, including guides and recommendations in the area of collection development, programming, and teen participation.

The Journal of Youth Services in Libraries/JOYS
American Library Association
50 East Huron St.
Chicago, IL 60611

This official publication of the Association for Library Service to Children (ALSC) and the Young Adult Library Services Association (YALSA) is a terrific resource for librarians working with children and young adults. It showcases current practices as well as spotlights activities and programs of both divisions.

MTV
http://www.mtv.com

If you want to find out what's hot in the music world from the number-one music television station, this is the place to visit. It doubles as a great collection development resource.

National Youth Development Information Center (NYDIC)
1319 F St. NW, Ste. 601
Washington, DC 20004
877-NYDIC-4-U   Fax: 202-393-4517
E-mail: info@nydic.org
Fax-on-Demand service: 888-653-6177
http://www.nydic.org/nydic/

NYDIC provides practice-related information about youth development to national and local youth-serving organizations at low cost or no cost.

React
http://www.react.com

React.com supports and celebrates teens' involvement in every aspect of their world, including news, celebrities, volunteering, shopping, relationship advice, fun, and homework resources. This site actively involves teens and celebrates their views and voices. It offers opportunities to post comments, rank and rate products and issues, share advice, enter contests, and answer surveys. Teen writing, reviews, and comments are posted regularly.

Search Institute
700 S. Third St., Ste. 210
Minneapolis, MN 55415
800-888-7828 or 612-376-8955
Fax: 612-376-8956
http://www.search-institute.org

The Search Institute is an independent, nonprofit, nonsectarian organization whose mission is to advance the well being of adolescents and children by generating knowledge and promoting its application. The web site is a great place for gathering information on teen needs and their development.

Teen
http://www.teen.com

To get the "scoop" on beauty, college, entertainment, and fashion, check out this site for teens. It's filled with surveys, interactive games and quizzes, homework help, e-zines, and teen journals and poetry.

Teen Ink
http://www.teenink.com

Teen Ink is a web site, a monthly print magazine, and a book series. In particular, the web site includes photos, teen issues, favorites lists, a teen art gallery, and reviews of music, movies, books. Everything here is written by teens for teens.

Teen Refuge
http://www.teenrefuge.com

Another web site to spark ideas for your teen area. Teen Refuge serves as a place for young adults to relax, have fun, meet other teens, and share ideas, concerns, and helpful advice.

Urban Libraries Council, Public Libraries as Partners in Youth Development
http://www.urbanlibraries.org/youth

This site is packed with everything "young adult" in public libraries. Schools will want to check it out too.

What Do Young Adults Read Next?: A Reader's Guide to Fiction for Young Adults, vols. 1–5. Detroit: Gale, 1994–2002.

A comprehensive readers advisory for young adult literature. By identifying similarities in various books, this selection guide helps readers and librarians choose titles of interest.

Planning, Space Needs, and Budget

American Libraries
50 E. Huron St.
Chicago, IL 60611

The April issue each year showcases new and renovated library facilities. This is quite an inspirational resource.

The American Library Association (ALA)
Young Adult Library Services Association (YALSA)
    http://www.ala.org/yalsa
American Association of School Libraries (AASL)
    http://www.ala.org/aasl
    50 E. Huron St.
    Chicago, IL 60611
    800-545-2433   Fax: 312-664-7459

Terrific resources for collection development, state and local young adult news, grants and awards, and much more. Find links to Teen Hoopla: An Internet Guide for Teens and to professional resources and publications, including *Young Adults Deserve the Best: Competencies for Librarians Serving Youth* (revised edition), 1998.

Americans with Disabilities Act (ADA)
    U.S. Department of Justice Civil Rights Div.,
    Disability Rights Sect., NYAVE
    950 Pennsylvania Ave. NW
    Washington, DC 20530
    800-514-0301   TTY: 800-514-0383
    http://www.usdoj.gov/crt/ada/adahom1.htm

ADA Standards for Accessible Design, as published in the Code of Federal Regulations, is available on the ADA web site in both HTML and PDF formats and with graphics, links to figures, and cross-referenced sections. A free CD-ROM containing a complete collection of ADA materials including architectural design standards, regulations, etc., is also available.

Cochran, Sally, and Peter Gisolfi. "Renovate It and They Will Come: Designing a Popular High School Library." *School Library Journal* 43, no. 2 (1997): 25–9.

Good school facilities planning resource. Based on the renovation of the library media center at the Horace Greeley High School in Chappaqua, New York.

Complete Home Designer or Complete Interior Designer (CD-ROMs). Needham Heights, Mass.: Data Becker.

Both products offer a complete range of options for designing and decorating in 3-D. Look for updated versions released every few years.

Connecticut State Library
    231 Capitol Ave.
    Hartford, CT 06106
    860-757-6500
    http://www.cslib.org

Good resource for information on library space planning. Includes guides and worksheets.

Connecting Young Adults and Libraries Website
    http://www.connectingya.com

Need information on teens and libraries? If so, this is the place to visit. Pay particular attention to the section called "Showing You the Money," which includes links to fifty-two funding resources.

Dahlgren, Anders C. *Public Library Space Needs: A Planning Outline.* Madison, Wis.: Wisconsin Dept. of Public Instruction, 1998.

Excellent space planning guide with ready-to-use worksheets.

Erickson, Rolf, and Carolyn Markuson. *Designing a School Library Media Center for the Future.* Chicago: American Library Assn., 2000.

Highly recommended for those who are involved in the design of a new school library or the renovation of an old one. Public librarians might also find it worth their time to take a look at this book.

Fraley, Ruth A., and Carol Lee Anderson. *Library Space Planning: A How-to-Do-It Manual for Assessing, Allocating and Reorganizing Collections, Resources and Facilities.* New York: Neal-Schuman, 1990.

How-to manual for all aspects of library space planning.

Home Depot
http://www.homedepot.com

General planning and decorating resource. Especially useful for getting help calculating carpeting, drywall, paint, and wallpaper.

Homestore.com
http://www.homestore.com/

Helpful planning and decorating information. One of the best features is the online room planner. Go directly to http://www.homestore.com/Decorate/Multimedia/Room_Planner for a quick and easy way to visualize your potential layout.

Library Journal
245 W. 17th St.
New York, NY 10011

Each year's December issue features an array of new library buildings, an annual buyer's guide, and a web site directory of vendors. Food for thought.

National Clearinghouse for Educational Facilities
http://www.edfacilities.org/ir/libraries.cfm

Resource list of links, books, and journal articles on the design of K–12 school libraries, including sample city and state guidelines and technology requirements.

Nelson, Sandra. *The New Planning for Results: A Streamlined Approach.* Chicago: American Library Assn., 2001.

This helpful publication assists libraries of all sized budgets to prepare for change.

The New York Library Association's (NYLA) Youth
Services Section (YSS)
252 Hudson Ave.
Albany, NY 12210-1802
800-252-6952 or 518-432-6952
Fax: 518-427-1697
http://www.nyla.org

Includes information on *The Key to the Future: Revised Minimum Standards for Youth Services in Public Libraries of New York State* and *The Basic Young Adult Services Handbook.*

Nichols, Mary Anne, and C. Allen, eds. *Young Adults and Public Libraries: A Handbook for Materials and Services.* Westport, Conn.: Greenwood, 1998.

A collection of articles by experts in the field of young adult services. Includes information helpful to those planning for young adult areas. Among the topics discussed: collection building (including magazines and nonprint materials), training teen staff, providing homework assistance programs, and confronting challenges of intellectual freedom, trends, and technology.

Planning and Building Libraries
http://www.slais.ubc.ca/resources/architecture/index3.html

This site was created for architects, librarians, and design consultants. Its primary purpose is to provide its users with an outline of design-related resources.

Ramos, Theresa. "From the Outside In: Library Renovations from the Perspectives of a Project Manager, an Architect/Designer, and a Technology Consultant." *Journal of Youth Services in Libraries* 14, no. 2 (winter 2001), 9.

Get tips and suggestions for working with outside consultants in renovation and new construction library projects.

The University of British Columbia School of Library, Archival, and Information Studies
http://www.slais.ubc.ca/resources/architecture/planning.html

Created for architects, librarians, and design consultants interested in planning and building libraries. Includes general planning guidelines for specific types of libraries, sample plans, and more.

Vaillancourt, Renée J. *Bare Bones Young Adult Services: Tips for Public Library Generalists,* 2d ed. Chicago: American Library Assn., 2000.

Fantastic resource for anyone interested in serving teens. Includes information on teen spaces and planning.

Voice of Youth Advocates
Scarecrow Press
4720 Boston Way
Lanham, MD 20706
888-486-9297

Published bimonthly. Starting in June 1999, each issue includes a "YA Spaces of Your Dreams" article featuring teen spaces from libraries across the United States. Helpful for both planning and designing, these articles outline the communities and planning processes along with descriptions and photos of teen areas. Also includes helpful information on teen programming, collection development, and more.

Wisconsin Department of Public Instruction
http://www.dpi.state.wi.us/dpi/dltcl/pld/plspace.html

A terrific space-planning resource with easy-to-use guides and worksheets. For worksheets, go to the "Appendices" and then click on D: Space Needs Worksheet (Excel file).

Interior Design and Decoration

American Society of Interior Designers
http://www.interiors.org

Useful resource for selecting and working with a professional designer. Also includes links to vendors, design-related information, and more.

Better Homes and Gardens Online
http://www.bhglive.com

A good general decorating and ideas web site that includes articles, plans, and useful tools. Supplement the online resource with the magazine for additional helpful tips and inspiration.

Better Homes and Gardens Paint Ideas & Decorating Techniques. Des Moines, Iowa: Better Homes and Gardens Books, 2000.

Includes how-tos for a variety of techniques including, for example, faux textiles, sponged-stamped bricks, color wash, tape stripes, and checkerboards. The author includes skill level, time, supplies, helpful hints, and step-by-step photographic instructions for each technique.

The Big Book of Teen Rooms. Little Rock, Ark.: Leisure Arts, 2001.

This guide to decorating teen bedrooms is advertised as "everything you need to create the 'perfect' room for your teen," and it's absolutely true. This book is a gem for generating thematic and other teen-friendly ideas.

Bolan, Kimberly, and Lisa C. Wemett. "Makeover Madness: Tips for Revamping Your Young Adult Area." *Voice of Youth Advocates* 22, no. 5 (Dec. 1999): 322–3.

Quick solutions for making over any teen area.

Cohen, Sacha. *The Practical Encyclopedia of Paint Recipes, Paint Effects and Special Finishes.* London, England: Hermes House, 2001.

Features more than 50 different treatments and expert advice. Techniques are clearly explained through informative text and step-by-step color photographs.

Decorating 1-2-3: Faux Painting, Wallpapering, Window Ttreatments, Floors, Molding and Trim, and Lighting Step-by-step. Des Moines, Iowa: Meredith, 2000.

Strong points of this publication include good color information and creative project ideas using decorative objects and materials. It also includes instructions for faux finishing, lighting installation, and other simple projects.

DecoratorsSecrets.com
http://www.decoratorsecrets.com

Home decorating ideas and tips on interior design and decorating on a budget with plenty of ideas that can be adapted to teens.

Doityourself.com
www.doityourself.com

Jam-packed with decorating information such as finding a contractor, obtaining free estimates, and much more.

Faux Fun: Painted Wall Finishes Made Easy (VHS), 1990, and *Faux Fun 2: Before and After* (VHS), 1999. Long Beach, Calif.: Faux Fun Videos.

Easy-to-follow, step-by-step video demonstrating different faux finishes for walls and decorative objects.

Gill, Martha. *Color Harmony for Interior Design.* Gloucester, Mass.: Rockport, 2001.

Packed with decorating tips, color swatches and palettes, advice, and color combinations, this book is a great guide to understanding color. Decorating tips show you how to choose and use color, including advice on selecting fabrics, paint, furniture, and accessories.

Heim, Judy, and Gloria Hansen. *Free Stuff for Home Decor on the Internet.* Concord, Calif.: C&T, 2000.

Whatever you need help with, this book will help you find it. Contains information on walls, windows, floors, and furniture as well as web sites associated with television shows, radio programs, and magazines.

House and Garden TV
http://www.hgtv.com

An excellent general resource for design and decorating tips, ideas, and suggested vendors.

Lord, Gary, and David Schmidt. *Marvelous Murals You Can Paint*. Cincinnati, Ohio: North Light, 2001.

Completely illustrated step-by-step techniques. Includes everything from simple projects to more-elaborate murals. The book is filled with tips and tricks for great results.

Maflin, Andrea. *Makeover Magic: Stylish Ideas to Transform Your Home on a Budget*. London, England: CIMA, 2000.

A fresh approach to decorating that can easily be applied to teen areas. Has step-by-step projects, decorating tips, and a variety of color photos.

Teen Room Décor Guide Picks
http://interiordec.about.com/cs/
teenroomdecor1/index.htm

Includes links for decorating rooms for older kids and teens. See photos and get do-it-yourself projects, thematic ideas, and tips.

Usalis, Marian D. "The Power of Paint: Refurbishing School Libraries on a Budget." *School Library Journal* 44, no. 2 (Feb. 1998): 28–33.

Funded by a grant, twenty-four elementary- and middle-school libraries in the Cleveland, Ohio, area were refurbished on approximately $5,000 per school. The results are friendly and exciting media centers.

USG Corp.
125 S. Franklin St.
Chicago, IL 60606-4678
800-874-4968
http://www.usg.com

Manufacturer of construction and remodeling building materials provides on this site technical information geared toward the professional designer, but if you can get past that, you'll find some very interesting ideas for ceilings and flooring.

Wrigley, Lynette. *Trompe l'oeil: Murals and Decorative Wall Painting*. New York: Rizzoli, 1997.

There are several trompe l'oeil books on the market, but this one is a treasure. It includes many new ideas and inspiring images as well as a discussion on painting techniques and issues of perspective.

Furniture, Fixtures, and Accessories

Allposters.com
http://www.allposters.com

The world's largest poster and print store.

Architectural Products by Outwater, L.L.C.
http://www.archpro.com

Extensive web resource for building and remodeling ideas catering to the special needs of builders, remodelers, and architects.

Brodart Co.
500 Arch St.
Williamsport, PA 17705
800-233-8467 (for books) or 888-820-4377
(for supplies and furnishings)
http://www.brodart.com

A familiar library vendor with progressive ideas for teens. Check out its web site under Library Supplies and Furnishings to find products for young adult areas, including an entire page dedicated to teen furniture and lounge-style seating. Also a great resource for library supplies, equipment, and display fixtures.

Corman & Assoc., Inc.
881 Floyd Dr.
Lexington, KY 40505
606-233-0544
http://www.cormans.com

Custom-manufactured fixtures, displays, props, and exhibits. Call to inquire about its CD catalog with thousands of items, an excellent design and idea resource.

Demco, Inc.
P.O. Box 7488
Madison, WI 53707
800-356-1200
http://www.demco.com

Although a traditional library vendor, Demco offers many great ideas for fixtures, including brochure racks, literature holders, and paperback spinners. Additional items to consider include spine labels, audiovisual and computer equipment, signage, and furniture. When it comes to furniture, be creative and look for items that say "teen."

Gaylord Brothers
P.O. Box 4901
Syracuse, NY 13221
800-448-6160
http://www.gaylord.com

A company specializing in libraries with ideas for display fixtures, shelving, supplies, and furnishings. Its furniture is rather traditional, so remember to "think teen" as you browse its catalog and web page.

Gifts In Kind International
333 N. Fairfax St.
Alexandria, VA 22314
703-836-2121   Fax: 703-549-1481
http://www.giftsinkind.org

Gifts In Kind International is a charitable organization that provides products, goods, and services from the private sector to the nonprofit sector. There are more than 350 Gifts In Kind affiliates worldwide. Free goods include, but are not limited to, furniture, computer equipment, paint, lighting fixtures, household goods, and office supplies and equipment.

Highsmith, Inc.
P.O. Box 800
Fort Atkinson, WI 53538-0800
800-558-2110
http://www.highsmith.com

Another traditional library vendor with some great products, including display units (small and large, wall-mounted and room dividers), cork rails, furnishings (look for "teen-friendly" items), sign solutions, and more.

Martin Brattrud, Inc.
1224 W. 132nd St.
Gardena, CA 90247
323-770-4147
http://www.martinbrattrud.com

A furniture manufacturer with stylish and comfortable ideas.

Metropolitan Furniture Co.
1635 Rollins Rd.
Burlingame, CA 94010
650-697-7900   Fax: 650-697-2818
http://www.metrofurniture.com

A furniture designer and manufacturer specializing in comfort and style. Its code is "design rules, authenticity matters, keep fresh!"

Pier 1 Imports
http://www.pierone.com

Unusual furnishings (including butterfly chairs), unique decorating accessories, pillows, and more.

Sauder Manufacturing
930 W. Barre Rd.
Archbold, OH 43502-0230
800-537-1530   Fax: 419-446-3697
http://www.sauderofficeworks.com/ and
    http://www.sauder.com

Manufacturer of wooden library tables and chairs. Multiple chair designs and fabric choices allow you to blend Sauder products with the rest of the library environment. The "3 Position Chair" is a clear winner for both computer and reading usage. Also look at its home furnishings, especially the "QBits" modular furniture systems.

Specialty Store Services
6115 Monroe Ct.
Morton Grove, IL 60053
800-999-0771
http://www.specialtystoreservices.com

Creative shelving and display ideas including mini grid cubes, various natural wood displays, creative lighting alternatives, and much more. The company's great signage ideas include motion message displays, neon-like illuminated signs, and backlit signs. It will even custom-design signs and banners. Visit online or request a free catalog.

Target, Inc.
http://www.target.com

A great alternative resource to traditional library furniture vendors with affordable furnishings, accessories, games, computer equipment, and electronics.

The Video Store Shopper
21707 Nordoff St.
Chatsworth, CA 91311
800-325-6867 or 818-717-8700
http://www.shopperinc.com

Excellent for original shelving (grid, slat wall, etc.) and display ideas, including a wide variety of media products and accessories. Send for a catalog to see creative alternatives for labels, lighting, and poster frames. You can even purchase celebrity stand-ups.

Marketing and Merchandising

Display and Design Ideas
http://www.ddimagazine.com

Product news and design solutions for store planning and visual merchandising.

Gail Junion-Metz, Information Age Consultants
E-mail: gail@iage.com
http://www.iage.com

Valuable resource for information on designing web sites for teens.

Jones, Patrick, and Joel Shoemaker. *Do It Right!: Best Practices for Serving Young Adults in School and Public Libraries.* New York: Neal-Schuman, 2001.

Guide for both public and school librarians that takes a customer service approach to serving young adults.

Jones, Patrick. "A Cyber-Room of Their Own: How Libraries Use Web Pages to Attract Young Adults." *School Library Journal* 43, no. 11 (Nov. 1997): 34–7.

A quick overview of how to create successful library web sites for teens. Emphasis is placed on attractive design, definition of the target audience, interesting content, and teen involvement.

Moses, Elissa. *The $100 Billion Allowance: Assessing the Global Teen Market.* New York: Wiley, 2000.

Helpful marketing and advertising tool for professionals targeting teens. Provides helpful information for understanding their similarities and differences as well as the results of a survey revealing teens' attitudes, values, and views.

Northern Sun Merchandising
2916 E. Lake St.
Minneapolis, MN 55406
800-258-8579
http://www.northersun.com

Specializing in message-oriented stickers, posters, buttons, t-shirts, magnets, and more.

Pew Internet and American Life Project
1100 Connecticut Ave. NW, Ste. 710
Washington, DC 20036
202-296-0019   Fax: 202-296-6797
http://www.pewinternet.org

Terrific resource for learning about the impact of the Internet on children, families, communities, schools, and more. An authoritative source for timely information on the Internet's growth and societal impact.

School Libraries on the Web
http://www.sldirectory.com

This site indexes K–12 school library web pages. You can quickly see how school library media centers are promoting themselves on the web.

Sudanco, Inc.
3217 Crites St.
Fort Worth, TX 76118-6236
817-589-7072
http://www.sudanco.com

Alternative company for classification and genre labels. Their "no-res" labels are fantastic, and their specialty is customization and problem solving.

Sullivan, Edward T. "Teenagers Are Not Luggage." *Public Libraries* 40, no. 2 (April 2001): 75–7.

Wonderful commentary on "what can be done for teens instead of what can be done about them." Includes a helpful list of additional resources for those serving young adults.

Virtual YA Index
http://www.suffolk.lib.ny.us/youth/virtual.html

This A-to-Z index of public library web pages provides a simple way to check out how public libraries are marketing to teens on the web.

Zollo, Peter. *Wise Up to Teens: Insights into Marketing and Advertising to Teenagers.* Ithaca, N.Y.: New Strategist, 1999.

Top-of-the-line teen marketing resource, including easy-to-use tables of data, insights, and real-life examples. Major topics covered include products, brands, media, activities, interests, trends, social hierarchy, music, celebrities, values, the essence of being teens, and teen life.

Resource Libraries

The following libraries are excellent resources for learning more about designing teen spaces, teen involvement, and marketing to teens.

Library/Address/Contact	Pop. Served	Est. Teen Pop.	Est. Teen Vols.	Teen Space Sq. Ft.	Teen Space Name	Result of
Allen County Public Library 900 Webster St. Fort Wayne, IN 46802 http://www.acpl.lib.in.us *Contact:* Edith Cummings, asst. mgr. of YA serv.	300,836	4,500	45,000	4,450	Young Adults Services	Redesign
Berkeley Public Library 2090 Kittredge St. Berkeley, CA 94704 http://www.infopeople.org/bpl *Contact:* Francisca Goldsmith, sr. libr. for teen serv.	105,000	4,000	N/A*	640	N/A	Renovation/ redesign
Brooklyn Public Library Central Library Grand Army Plz. Brooklyn, NY 11238 http://www.brooklynpub liclibrary.org	N/A	N/A	N/A	N/A	N/A	N/A
Campbell County Public Library 2101 4 J Road Gillette, WY 82718 http://www.ccpls.org *Contact:* Susan Knesel, YA serv. mgr.	30,000	3,200	8,254	940	Young Adult Area and Teen Room	Renovation/ redesign

*N/A = Not available *or* not applicable

Library/Address/Contact	Est. Pop. Served	Est. Teen Pop.	Est. Teen Vols.	Teen Space Sq. Ft.	Space Name	Result of
Carmel High School Library, 520 E. Main St. Carmel, IN 46032 http://www.ccs.k12.in.us/chs *Contact:* Bonnie Grimble, library media dir.	3,500	3,500	30,000	26,000	N/A	New construction
Chicago Ridge Public Library 10400 S. Oxford Ave. Chicago Ridge, IL 60415 http://chicagoridge.lib.il.us *Contact:* Constance VanSwol, youth serv. libr.	13,750	1,500	1,000	400	*Café Read*	Redesign
Chino Hills Branch Library 2003 Grand Ave. Chino Hills, CA 91709 http://www.discover.net/ ~library *Contact:* Leonard Hernandez, YA specialist	66,787	11,304	6,420	900	Extreme Teen Center	Renovation/ redesign
Fort Vancouver Regional Library District 1007 E. Mill Plain Blvd. Vancouver, WA 98663 http://205.238.52.5 *Contact:* Tricia Segal, coord. of YA serv.	N/A	N/A	N/A	N/A	N/A	N/A
Garfield Park Branch Santa Cruz City–County Public Libraries 705 Woodrow Ave. Santa Cruz, CA 95060 http://63.193.16.16 or http://63.193.16.16/grant_ manual/index.html *Contact:* Janis O'Driscoll, coord. of youth serv.	N/A	N/A	N/A	N/A	N/A	N/A
Haslett Public Library 5670 School St. Haslett, MI 48840 http://www.cadl.org/branches/ Haslett_library.htm *Contact:* Amy Brown, lib. asst.	10,230	3,207	750	100	The Teen Area	Redesign

Library/Address/Contact	Est. Pop. Served	Est. Teen Pop.	Est. Teen Vols.	Teen Space Sq. Ft.	Space Name	Result of
Jackson County Library Services' Central Library 413 W. Main St. Medford, OR 97501 *Contact:* Christine Perkins, teen library coord.	70,000	N/A	N/A	500	The Teen Library	Renovation/ redesign
King County Library System Administrative Offices 960 Newport Way NW Issaquah, WA 98027 425-369-3200 http://www.kcls.org	42 libraries	N/A	N/A	N/A	N/A	N/A
Lake Hills Library King County Library System 15228 Lake Hills Blvd. Bellevue, WA 98007 http://www.kcls.org/lh/home. html *Contact:* Sally Porter, youth coord.	N/A	N/A	N/A	500	The Teen Zone	Renovation/ redesign
Laramie County Library System 2800 Central Ave. Cheyenne, WY 82001 http://www.lclsonline.org *Contact:* Amelia Shelley, children and teen serv. mgr.	93,000	7,000	27,000	100	N/A	N/A
Lawrence Public Library 707 Vermont St. Lawrence, KS 66044 http://www.lawrence.lib.ks.us *Contact:* Kimberly Patton, YA specialist	72,721	12,914	6,800	600	The Zone	Redesign
Leominster Public Library 30 West St. Leominster, MA 01453 *Contact:* Diane Sanabria, YA serv. coord.	40,208	N/A	2,500	768	Robert Cormier Center for Young Adults	Renovation/ redesign
Los Angeles Public Library 630 W. Fifth St. Los Angeles, CA 90071 http://www.lapl.org/teenscape *Contact:* Georgette Todd, dir. of YA serv.	3,800,000	300,000	30,000	4,000	Teen'Scape	New construction and renovation

Library/Address/Contact	Est. Pop. Served	Est. Teen Pop.	Est. Teen Vols.	Teen Space Sq. Ft.	Space Name	Result of
Marion Public Library P.O. Box 30 Marion, NY 14505 http://www.marion.pls-net.org *Contact:* Pamela Wolfanger, library mgr.	4,901	500–700	500 (fiction)	99	Café Read	New construction
Mentor Public Library 8215 Mentor Ave. Mentor, OH 44060 http://www.mentorpl.org *Contact:* Cheryl Kuonen, head of YA serv.	N/A	N/A	N/A	N/A	N/A	N/A
Mercer County Library System Lawrence Headquarters 2751 Brunswick Pike Lawrenceville, NJ 08648 http://www.mcl.org *Contact:* Laura Gruniger, YA libr.	4,376	1,059	6,526	773	None	Redesign
North Central H.S. Information Center 1801 E. 86th St. Indianapolis, IN 46240 http://www.msdwt.k12.in.us/schools/NC/Ncentral.htm *Contact:* Sue Landaw, info. ctr. dept. chair	3,300	3,300	50,000	55,000	Information Center	Renovation/redesign
North Country School P.O. Box 187 Cascade Rd. Lake Placid, NY 12946 http://www.nct.org/school *Contact:* Alison Follos, libr.	75	75	3,500	N/A	N/A	Redesign
Peabody Institute Library 82 Main St. Peabody, MA 01960 http://www.peabodylibrary.org *Contact:* Kelley Rae Brown, YA libr.	49,212	9,571	5,154	1,332	YA Café	Renovation/redesign
Phelps Community Memorial Library 15 Church St. Phelps, NY 14532 http://www.phelps.pls-net.org *Contact:* Kimberly Taney (see Webster Public Library)	7,017	1,066	753 (fiction)	140	None	Renovation/redesign

Library/Address/Contact	Est. Pop. Served	Est. Teen Pop.	Est. Teen Vols.	Teen Space Sq. Ft.	Space Name	Result of

Phoenix Public Library
  1221 N. Central Ave.
  Phoenix, AZ 85004
  http://www.phoenixlibrary.
   org/web/teens
Contact: Elaine Meyers, children's and teen serv. mgr.
	1,321,045	196,896	10,000	5,000	Teen Central	New construction

Pioneer Library System
  4595 Rte. 21 N
  Canandaigua, NY 14424
  http://www.pls-net.org
Contact: Jennifer Morris, exec. dir.
	42 libraries	N/A	N/A	N/A	N/A	N/A

The Saginaw Libraries
  505 Janes Ave.
  Saginaw, MI 48607
  http://www.saginaw.lib.mi.us
Contact: Rhonda Butler, children's and youth serv. coord.
	N/A	N/A	N/A	N/A	N/A	N/A

San Antonio Public Library
  600 Soledad
  San Antonio, TX 78205
  http://www.sanantonio.gov/
   library
Contact: Adriana Flores Heard, YA libr.; Jennifer Comi, dept.mgr.
	1,185,394	10,000	6,580	3,500	youth (wired)	Redesign and renovation

San Joaquin Valley Library System
  Fresno County Public Library
  (Headquarters)
  2420 Mariposa St.
  Fresno, CA 93721
  http://www.sjvls.lib.ca.us
Contact: Kelley Worman, head of youth services
	2,098,773	151,112	N/A	N/A	N/A	N/A

Santa Cruz City–County Public Libraries
  System Headquarters
  1543 Pacific Ave.
  Santa Cruz, CA 95060
  http://www.santacruzpl.org
	10 branches and a bookmobile	N/A	N/A	N/A	N/A	N/A

Library/Address/Contact	Est. Pop. Served	Est. Teen Pop.	Est. Teen Vols.	Teen Space Sq. Ft.	Space Name	Result of
Schaumburg Township District Library 130 S. Roselle Rd. Schaumburg, IL 60193 http://www.stdl.org *Contact:* Amy Alessio, teen coord.	150,000	11,000	1,900	750	Teen Center	Renovation/ redesign
Swampscott Public Library 61 Burrill St. Swampscott, MA 01907 http://www.noblenet.org/ swampscott *Contact:* Vicky Pratt Coffin, reference and YA libr.	13,464	1,340	1,200	162	The Teen Area	Redesign
Union County Public Library W. Main St. Lake Butler, FL 32054 http://union.newriver.lib.fl. us/junior.htm *Contact:* Nick Burke, CLA dir.	13,000	700	400	500	N/A	N/A
Webster Public Library 980 Ridge Rd. Webster, NY 14580 http://www.websterlibrary. org *Contact:* Kimberly Bolan Taney, network and patron serv. dir.; Lisa C. Wemett, asst. dir. and teen serv. libr.	34,000	3,867	3,704	1,500	The Teen Lounge	New con- struction

Index

Kimberly Bolan Taney is the network administrator and patron services librarian at the Webster (New York) Public Library. Taney served as the young adult specialist/project coordinator in the Pioneer Library System (Canandaigua, New York), where she worked on a grant to assist rural public libraries in designing their teen spaces. She is an independent young adult consultant on young adult services and teen space design. A presenter at PLA national conferences and a former consultant to the Kentucky Department for Libraries and Archives on a state-wide teen services project, Taney contributed to the New York Library Association's publication *The Basic Young Adult Services Handbook* and has written articles for *VOYA*. Recently, she has designed new teen spaces for the Webster and Marion (New York) Public Libraries.